MISSION: ORGANIZATION

STRATEGIES AND SOLUTIONS TO CLEAR YOUR CLUTTER

MEREDITH® BOOKS
DES MOINES, IOWA

HGTV MISSION: ORGANIZATION

EDITOR Amy Tincher-Durik
ART DIRECTOR Chad Jewell
CONTRIBUTING WRITERS Jody Garlock, Susan Kleinman
COPY CHIEF Terri Fredrickson
PUBLISHING OPERATIONS MANAGER Karen Schirm
EDIT AND DESIGN PRODUCTION COORDINATOR Mary Lee Gavin
EDITORIAL ASSISTANTS Kaye Chabot, Kairee Windsor
MARKETING PRODUCT MANAGERS Aparna Pande, Isaac Petersen, Gina Rickert, Stephen Rogers, Brent Wiersma, Tyler Woods
BOOK PRODUCTION MANAGERS Pam Kvitne, Marjorie J. Schenkelberg, Rick von Holdt, Mark Weaver
CONTRIBUTING COPY EDITOR Jane Woychick
CONTRIBUTING PROOFREADERS Genelle Deist, Becky Etchen, Beth Havey
CONTRIBUTING PHOTOGRAPHERS David Buttigieg (Anyway Productions Inc.), Scott Little, Nigel Marson, Blaine Moats, Alexandra Rowley (Anyway Productions Inc.), Paul Whicheloe (Anyway Productions Inc.)
CONTRIBUTING STYLISTS Christa Bianchi, Jenny Key Baker, Kellie Kramer
INDEXER Elizabeth Parson

MEREDITH. BOOKS

EXECUTIVE DIRECTOR, EDITORIAL Gregory H. Kayko
EXECUTIVE DIRECTOR, DESIGN Matt Strelecki
EXECUTIVE EDITOR/GROUP MANAGER Denise Caringer
SENIOR ASSOCIATE DESIGN DIRECTOR Doug Samuelson

PUBLISHER AND EDITOR IN CHIEF James D. Blume
EDITORIAL DIRECTOR Linda Raglan Cunningham
EXECUTIVE DIRECTOR, MARKETING Jeffrey B. Myers
EXECUTIVE DIRECTOR, NEW BUSINESS DEVELOPMENT Todd M. Davis
EXECUTIVE DIRECTOR, SALES Ken Zagor
DIRECTOR, OPERATIONS George A. Susral
DIRECTOR, PRODUCTION Douglas M. Johnston
BUSINESS DIRECTOR Jim Leonard

VICE PRESIDENT AND GENERAL MANAGER Douglas J. Guendel

MEREDITH PUBLISHING GROUP

PRESIDENT Jack Griffin
SENIOR VICE PRESIDENT Bob Mate

MEREDITH CORPORATION

CHAIRMAN AND CHIEF EXECUTIVE OFFICER William T. Kerr
PRESIDENT AND CHIEF OPERATING OFFICER Stephen M. Lacy

IN MEMORIAM E. T. Meredith III (1933–2003)

Copyright © 2004 by Meredith Corporation, Des Moines, Iowa. First Edition.
All rights reserved. Printed in the United States of America.
Library of Congress Control Number: 2004110684
ISBN: 0-696-22284-1

All of us at Meredith® Books are dedicated to providing you with information and ideas to enhance your home. We welcome your comments and suggestions. Write to us at: Meredith Books, Home Decorating and Design Editorial Department, 1716 Locust St., Des Moines, IA 50309-3023.

If you would like to purchase any of our home decorating and design, cooking, crafts, gardening, or home improvement books, check wherever quality books are sold. Or visit us at: meredithbooks.com

For more information on the topics included in this book and the show *Mission: Organization*, visit HGTV.com/organized

All materials provided in this book by or on behalf of HGTV or otherwise associated with HGTV's program *Mission: Organization* are owned by Scripps Networks, Inc. and are used under license by Meredith Corporation. "HGTV," "Home and Garden Television," the HGTV logo, and the title "Mission: Organization" are service marks and/or trademarks of Scripps Networks, Inc.

Mission: Organization is produced by Nancy Glass Productions.

FOREWORD

People often ask me where the idea for *Mission: Organization* came from. Anyone who has ever seen the piles of paper on my desk or looked in my crammed coat closet knows the answer. I tend to drop things in a convenient spot and let everything pile up. Hats and gloves disappear into the abyss. Important documents become mixed with junk mail. I am the only adult I know who still uses mitten clips. The funny thing is, most of my house is very neat. Most of my office is very neat. But those few spots give me trouble.

I discovered I was not alone. People were always telling me that their friends or coworkers had the same problem. So I began to think: For a television company specializing in design shows, maybe the next great show was the pile on my desk. A program dedicated to examining and solving people's organizational problems could be both entertaining and enlightening.

Luckily HGTV felt the same way. But this was new television territory. How would the show work? My team decided *Mission: Organization* would find homeowners who were disorganized, examine how things got that way, then teach the homeowners how to cure their clutter problem for good. Then we thought about it some more and we began to worry. We didn't know if people would let us into their homes, let us see their mess, and reveal their vulnerabilities. It turned out there was nothing to worry about. People who collect clutter are acutely aware of their problem, especially when they are tripping over it. Homeowners and their families welcomed us in because they were ready for a change—and we were able to help them make it. Best of all, the people we dealt with approached their disorganized mess with a sense of humor and a "get it done" spirit.

The families we have featured on the show are wonderful. They have all worked really hard to change their ways. "Yeah, but what happens after you leave?" we are often asked. We check up on our families and have found that, for the most part, they have kept it together. And we've discovered that organization is contagious: Many of the people actually want to attack other areas of clutter without any help.

Working on *Mission: Organization* has been a terrific experience. I have learned so much and I have begun to look at design in a different, more practical way. It appears I am not alone: Organization is one of the fastest-growing areas of design.

So am I neat and organized? Well, yes, I finally am. Now maybe I can give up those mitten clips.

Nancy Glass

NANCY GLASS
PRODUCER, MISSION: ORGANIZATION

CONTENTS

YOUR ALL-IN-ONE HANDBOOK FOR BRINGING ORDER TO YOUR HOME

When you walk through the front door after a long day of work, you toss your keys, coat, and bag on the floor, too tired to open the hall closet—and now your mate and kids have followed suit. Toys have taken over your kids' bedrooms and migrated into the living and dining rooms—forcing you to step over mountains of toys every time you want to watch TV or eat a meal. Your spouse loves tag sales, secondhand stores, and flea markets, and now your garage is in total disarray—filled with so many castoffs that you could start your own resale shop. Sound familiar? If so you aren't alone!

Keeping a home neat and organized on top of family and work obligations is no easy task. However, *HGTV Mission: Organization* can help. This book will teach you how to get your clutter under control and how to devise a system that works for you, your family, and your lifestyle. Along the way you will discover foolproof ideas from the professional organizers featured on the hit television show *Mission: Organization* and see real-life room transformations sure to inspire your own decluttering mission. Turn the page to learn more about the exciting features you'll find in this book.

BEFORE AFTER

See page 70 for this amazing apartment makeover.

See page 88 for more on this basement overhaul.

BEFORE

AFTER

NOAH

BEFORE AFTER

See page 80 for this great garage cleanup.

3 STEPS TO A SUCCESSFUL MISSION

When you undertake any organizational task, three key components come into play: sorting your possessions, storing what you keep, and—possibly the most important step—maintaining your organizational system. The goal of this section is to teach you a winning system for transforming even your most chaotic spaces into rooms that make you feel proud and relaxed, rooms that you can enjoy. In these pages you'll find invaluable tips for holding a successful tag sale (so you can turn what you no longer need into cash), choosing the right storage containers for your needs, and maintaining a clutter-free life. You'll also find great ideas for making your spaces—from small closets to huge basements—more functional and attractive.

A ROOM-BY-ROOM GUIDE TO CUTTING THE CLUTTER

Here you'll learn to put your three-step mission into action! This section includes ideas for sorting and storing the possessions in your kitchen, bathroom, living room, and more. It will instill you with good habits so that you can stay organized.

Once you put these ideas into practice, you will never again buy a bag of sugar only to find one buried at the back of your cupboard or deal with papers that have migrated from your designated living room office to the kitchen.

REAL HOMES, REAL CHALLENGES— AND REAL SOLUTIONS

Each week viewers watch as host Gail O'Neill introduces a home in need of decluttering and homeowners who need a little help achieving their organizational goals. Sometimes it's hard to comprehend how these homeowners have landed in such a predicament: you know, the garage that's overflowing with tag sale finds, gardening tools, and sports equipment; or the living room that's littered with paper, toys, and office equipment. However, almost everyone has at least one space that might look equally shocking on camera.

This section includes 12 actual homes featured on *Mission: Organization*. These case studies are organized by common problems and challenges. You will see garages, home offices, and more go from woeful to wonderful—and you will learn how to translate these examples to suit your own spaces and individual needs. You'll also get tips and ideas from the professional organizers who—armed with a plan and a little tough love—made these once-chaotic spaces hum with efficiency.

READY TO START YOUR MISSION?

If you've been putting off cleaning out your closet or straightening your living room, it's time to get started! Once you have made a commitment to organize your home, you're halfway to the goal. Working through the process of sorting and storing may be time-consuming, so pump up your motivation: Imagine the sense of accomplishment you will feel when you open a closet and all the contents don't spill onto the floor. Imagine relaxing in a well-organized living room. Then keep reading. This book will help you gain confidence in your ability to control clutter and teach you how to keep it out of your life for good. And that's a mission worth accomplishing.

3 STEPS TO A SUCCESSFUL MISSION

If you've seen the "before" and "after" scenes on HGTV's *Mission: Organization*—or if you have perused the case studies that are introduced on page 66—you know that even the most hopeless-looking, chaotic spaces *can* become clean and organized. Review and use the following steps as you begin your cleaning and organizing journey. Whether you're entering an unruly closet or clearing a path through your basement, they'll keep you moving forward.

1 SORT THINGS THROUGH

Before you can organize your belongings, you need to know exactly what you have and what's worth keeping. This book will show you how to sift through the contents of your closets, drawers, and more and help you decide what to keep and what to eliminate.

2 STORE YOUR STUFF

After you sift and sort your belongings, you'll need to store what you keep. Storage containers can be both beautiful and efficient, allowing you to find whatever you need whenever you need it. This book will help you assess the myriad organizing products and systems on the market so that you'll choose the best bins, boxes, and bags for your particular situation.

3 STAY ORGANIZED

Once your home is clutter-free, you may be tempted to sit back, put your feet up, and resume life as usual. You've earned the rest; however, "as usual" may result in a new jumble of junk six months from now. *HGTV Mission: Organization* will help you avoid that fate by teaching you how to set up systems that suit the way you think and the way you live. You'll learn how to stem the tide of clutter before it enters your home and how to manage your projects so that clutter has no chance to accumulate.

WHY ORGANIZE?

The initial process of organizing your home may be time-consuming. The transformations you see in half an hour on *Mission: Organization* can take professional organizers days—or even weeks—to accomplish. However, the results are well worth the effort! Consider this:

GETTING ORGANIZED
WILL SAVE YOU TIME

Are you often late for work because you spend an hour looking for your car keys? Is cooking dinner a chore because your pots and pans aren't easily accessible? Do homework assignments take all night to complete because your kids can't find the markers and glue sticks? Never again! After you complete your own Mission: Organization, you'll know exactly where your keys are, all your cooking supplies and ingredients will be within easy reach (bringing a whole new meaning to the phrase "fast food"), and homework assignments will be done in a snap.

GETTING ORGANIZED
WILL SAVE YOU MONEY

How many times have you bought something and then discovered two weeks later that you already had the same item buried at the bottom of your closet? And how many things have you discarded and replaced because improper storage left them crumpled or crushed beyond repair? An organized home will spare you those expenses. Finally, if you have so much stuff that you are paying for off-site storage, getting organized can save you hundreds of dollars every month.

GETTING ORGANIZED
WILL IMPROVE YOUR HEALTH

Are you stressed out? A disorganized life can be extremely stressful, and stress can wreak havoc on your body and your mind. What's more, clutter is a magnet for dust and other household allergens. When you get rid of the dust catchers, you may soon find that you're rid of headaches, sniffles, and your scratchy throat too.

GETTING ORGANIZED
WILL IMPROVE YOUR RELATIONSHIPS

Has clutter overtaken your life—and affected your relationships with your family and friends? Imagine how much more romantic your bedroom will be when the dressers are no longer covered with old magazines and the foot of the bed is no longer a dumping ground for yet-to-be-folded laundry. (Imagine too: no more bickering about who misplaced the dry cleaning ticket or the garage door opener!) Consider how much richer your life would be if you were comfortable inviting guests over more frequently or if you encouraged neighbors to drop by anytime. Picture sitting down to dinner with your family in an organized, inviting kitchen—and then envision your kids actually wanting to hang out with their friends at *your* house for a change. An organized home will allow you and your family to spend more time with one another and with friends—and you'll truly enjoy that time together.

GETTING ORGANIZED
WILL MAKE YOU HAPPIER

Does your cluttered home affect your mood? Once your home is clean and organized, you will feel better about yourself. You know that guilty feeling you have when you open your messy closet? You'll banish it forever. You know how uncomfortable you are when visitors arrive unannounced or on short notice? An organized home will guarantee that you rarely if ever have to say, "Please pardon the mess." And the feeling of accomplishment you will gain from successfully completing your own Mission: Organization will spill over into other areas of your life, making you feel more confident, more capable, and happier. Isn't that worth a weekend of your time and hard work?

PLAN TO SUCCEED

Are you ready to get started? Great! But before you tear apart that closet or empty those drawers, take some time to plan your organizing project, define your goals, and develop a strategy for succeeding. The time you put in up front will make your organizing mission more manageable and will help you avoid mistakes and unnecessary expenses.

CHOOSE YOUR MISSION

First decide which area of your home you want to organize. One closet? Your living room? If you break your overall mission into minimissions, the task at hand will seem far less overwhelming—and you will see success more quickly. Dividing your project into smaller pieces will also help ensure that you have enough time to complete each phase of the project. That's important because the only thing worse than a disorganized closet is an empty closet whose former contents sit in the middle of the floor for five months while you are sidetracked by other activities.

Next write a list of the functions your organized space needs to serve. Be specific. Identifying exactly how you need your home to work will help you organize each room in a way that makes sense for you. If you share a home with others, consult with the entire household to get a clear picture of everyone's needs. For a kitchen, for example, your "wish list" might include space for kids' breakfasts and snacks as well as a place for them to do their homework; or your list might also include a computer and printer niche for a home business, or a comfy chair for chatting on the phone. Similarly your living room may have to provide space for formal dining and a place for watching and storing videos and DVDs;

or you may need the room to moonlight as a homework zone or yoga studio. Remember: Organizing has no rigid rules. True organization means equipping and arranging a space in a manner that suits your own particular needs and your own lifestyle.

LIVING THROUGH THE MISSION

Once you have figured out where you are going to start and what you need to accomplish in that space, you'll have to attend to some practical preliminary matters. First consider how you are going to function without the chosen space while your mission is in progress. Will you be organizing the kitchen? Plan to eat out (in a restaurant or outside) on the days you're working in that room. Otherwise you'll have to interrupt the sorting of cooking utensils and clear them off the table so you can serve a meal. Then you'll have to do the dishes—and start the sorting all over again.

Organizing your kids' rooms? You may need to use their floors as a sorting station for toys. Can you arrange for your children to sleep over at a friend's house or organize a special sleepover in the family room? Otherwise you may be staring at 5,348 blocks at 9 p.m. while you wonder where and how to put your cranky kids down for the night.

You will also have to figure out where, when, and how you will dispose of garbage. When is trash pickup day in your neighborhood? And where can you keep your discards until then? Will you have to deliver any items to the dump yourself? (Check with your municipality.) If so will these items fit in your own car, or do you need to borrow a minivan or an SUV from a friend or neighbor?

GEARING UP

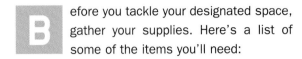

Before you tackle your designated space, gather your supplies. Here's a list of some of the items you'll need:

■ **Large garbage bags.** You'll be using these to dispose of things that neither you nor anyone else will ever use again. Buy more than you think you will need; you'll be amazed at how much garbage you will actually uncover. The heavy-duty black kind made for leaf and branch disposal are a good choice because they are less likely to rip than lighter, cheaper varieties.

■ **Cardboard cartons.** These are for items you will be donating, selling, or moving to another room in your house. Even if you have a mountain of stuff to store, choose boxes of a modest size so they'll be easy to lift when full.

■ **Latex or vinyl gloves.** Items that haven't been used for years are likely to be quite dusty, and all that dust can be hard on your skin. Wearing gloves will help you avoid allergies and rashes—and will minimize the chance of cuts and scrapes as well.

■ **A notebook and pen.** As you sort through your belongings, you will take inventory of the items you are keeping so that you can shop for organizing aids (see pages 25 to 30 for more information on choosing storage containers).

■ **Bottled water.** If you head to the kitchen every time you get thirsty, your organizing project will take longer to complete. Keep some bottled water at hand and sip throughout the day.

■ **Upbeat music.** You've got a long day or weekend ahead of you. Listening to music you enjoy will make the time pass more quickly—and the work may actually start to feel like fun!

SHIP 'EM OFF
Even if you're not going to be working in your kids' rooms, you may find it helpful to send them to visit a friend or relative while you get organized. You'll work more efficiently if you are not interrupted, and your sorted piles are more likely to stay intact without children around.

LISTEN TO THE PROS
Read this entire section before beginning your mission. It contains tricks the pros use to organize their own homes and the unruly rooms in their clients' homes. Once you understand the process of organizing you'll be able to create a strategy to tackle your project.

HELP IS ON THE WAY!
Having trouble tossing your stuff or organizing what you keep after a big clear-out? Hire a professional organizer. This service may pay for itself if it helps you eliminate the need for off-site storage. See page 35 for more information on finding a professional organizer in your area.

STEP 1
SORT THINGS THROUGH

SORTING YOUR STUFF

Now you are ready to get organized. Pages 38 to 65 provide tips for organizing specific areas of your home. No matter which room you wish to organize, the following principles apply: 1) To sort your belongings most efficiently, start at one end of the space and work your way to the other, resisting the temptation to bounce around. 2) Handle each item only once. Make a decision about each object as you go along and put each piece directly into the appropriate bin or bag. As you pick up each item, ask yourself:

■ **Is it garbage?** If so throw it out now. If you believe it is wasteful to get rid of things that are in perfectly good condition, consider this: Clutter costs you money, may make you sick, and may cause family friction. Now do you still want to hold on to that unused waffle iron?

■ **Does it need to be repaired?** If it is really worth repairing, put it in a box labeled "repair." If the cost of repairing the item is more than the item itself is worth, or if your family has outgrown the item, put it in the trash. Inexpensive repairs are no bargain if you have no use for an item.

■ **Has it been more than a year since anyone used this or enjoyed it?** Put it in a box labeled "give away/sell." Depending on the space you're organizing, these boxes will include clothes and toys your children have outgrown, equipment for sports or hobbies you no longer enjoy, duplicates of items you already own (no one needs three toasters), and books you will probably not reread. Jot down the contents of each box as you fill it. If you donate your unwanted items, you will need this inventory come tax time (see page 20 for more information).

■ **Do I use the item in a different room?** If so put it in a box labeled "relocate." You can move the contents of the box to other rooms at the end of the day.

■ **Is the item actually used and enjoyed in this room?** If so put it in the "keepers" pile.

SENTIMENTAL JOURNEYS

It can be tough to throw away or give away some pieces of your past. Before you place something with the "keepers," ask yourself the following:

■ **How do I really feel about the person who gave this to me?** When was the last time you thought about your high school sweetheart? Although you may want to hold on to a few special mementos, is it necessary to keep every letter, movie ticket stub, or gift?

■ **Can I save one and discard the rest?** How about discarding all but one of your grandmother's hankies? One will take up less room than a dozen and will help you preserve the memories without the mess.

■ **Can I find a new use for it?** If your Uncle Fred's Limoges teacups are sitting idle, put them to use. Line them up on your desk to hold paper clips, rubber bands, and pushpins. Use one on your bedside table to hold your watch while you sleep.

■ **Can this item help someone else?** It can be difficult to part with your wedding dress, your kids' baby clothes, or the reading glasses your mother wore to do the crossword puzzle every afternoon. However, imagine how useful these items could be if you donated them to a family in need. Your wedding dress could help another bride feel beautiful on her special day. Those old sleepers could keep a baby warm next winter. Your mother's glasses could help a struggling senior read the news or letters from a grandchild. Wouldn't that be a great way to honor your marriage or your loved ones?

AFTER THE SORTING

When you have finished sorting your stuff into piles, take the trash out of the room—and out of the house altogether if possible. Put the objects that need to be repaired in your car (on the front seat so that you don't forget about them) and resolve to drop them off at the tailor, repair shop, or shoemaker within a week. If you don't care enough about them to get them repaired in the next week, accept the fact that you don't really need them and toss them into the trash.

Next take the "relocate" box and walk through your house, putting each item away in the appropriate room. Then go through the "give away/sell" box and decide whether you want to sell or donate. The advantage of selling things, of course, is that your clutter can net some

cash. If you have many items with significant value to collectors, selling them may be quite profitable. If you don't have much marketable stuff, it may be simpler and more efficient to donate your things to a favorite charity.

SMOOTH SALE-ING

If you choose to sell the items you no longer use, consider whether you have enough to justify running a tag sale. A weekend-long tag sale that raises only $43 may not be the best use of your time. However, if you are ready to part with every toy your kids have outgrown in the past few years or four sets of dishes and an entire *batterie de cuisine*, a yard sale may pay off. Price items a little higher than the lowest price you're willing to accept and allow customers to bargain. All shoppers love feeling that they've received a good deal!

If you have a few pieces of fine furniture to sell, place an ad in your local newspaper. Interested customers can come and view the merchandise at your convenience. (Also visit www.craigslist.com for online classified ads in most major U.S. cities.) *Safety note: Do not allow strangers into your home when you are alone. Arrange for your spouse or another adult to be with you when customers come to call.*

If the items you have for sale are true collectibles, consider auctioning them online. Websites such as eBay give you access to millions of snow globe collectors or majolica aficionados around the world. Because of the time involved (from developing item descriptions to monitoring your auctions), it rarely pays to sell items worth only a few dollars. Remember: Time is money.

WHEN YOU CAN'T DECIDE

If you have been staring at an item, unable to decide whether to toss or keep it, ask yourself, "What's the worst thing that could possibly happen if I get rid of this?" Most of the time you'll realize that the negative consequences of keeping the object far outweigh any possible problems caused by throwing it away. As you sort, pay attention to your body. If you get a headache or feel a tightness in your chest whenever you look at a certain object, you probably need to eliminate that item from your life.

TAG SALE SMARTS

If you plan to have a tag sale (also known as a garage sale), evaluate your potential merchandise and decide whether you can make enough money to compensate for the time it will take you to organize the sale, mark the items, and work for the weekend. If you have enough stuff for a sale, the following tips will help you "sale" your way to success.

■ Spend a few weekends visiting tag sales in your area. See what items tend to sell and which tend to sit. Also look at prices to help you determine what your local market will bear. Avoid the temptation to purchase items at these sales. Remember you are aiming to clear your clutter, not add to it.

■ Set a date for your sale, noting where holidays and other community events fall on the calendar. While it probably isn't wise to hold a sale on a major holiday, it may be a good idea to sell your items when you'll attract a large crowd (for instance, during a citywide festival or community tag sale).

■ Present only clean and neat items for sale. Steam wrinkled clothes and wash grimy kitchenware—no one wants to buy a greasy skillet.

■ Check with your town government to see whether you need a permit. If a permit is required, evaluate how much it will cost; will the fee consume a large portion of what you intend to make at your sale?

■ Come up with a rain contingency plan. If the weather doesn't cooperate, will you hold the sale indoors? Postpone it? Cancel it?

■ Spread the word. If you have enough inventory to warrant the expense, place an ad in the local newspaper's classified section. Regardless of whether you advertise in the paper, post signs (with clear directions) on telephone poles and bulletin boards around town.

■ Make your yard safe for foot traffic. Anyone who trips on a divot or stumbles over an exposed pipe may have the right to seek legal action.

■ Place a price sticker on every item, or sort items by price and put them on tables marked "Everything $5," "Everything $10," and so on.

■ Stock up on change (coins and small bills) so that you can accept large bills.

■ An hour before you end the sale, post a sign proclaiming "everything must go" and lower the prices. At the end of the sale, gather the items that remain and either put them in your car to donate to a charity or toss them in the trash.

RALLY THE TROOPS

You've made the commitment to organize your home, and it's time to get the rest of the family on board. Perhaps—lucky you!—everyone else is as eager to get started as you are. However, if you are being met with resistance from your mate or children, you may have to come up with creative ways to motivate them. Here are some ideas:

■ Turn it into a contest. The person who throws out the most junk wins a special prize.

■ If you're planning a tag sale, allow each family member to keep the money earned from his or her items (or to spend the earnings on whatever he or she chooses).

■ Set a shared goal. If your family prefers working together rather than competing, hold a vote to decide how you'll celebrate (an outing? a visit to a favorite restaurant?) when the project is completed.

If these strategies fail, you may have to accept the fact that you are flying solo on this particular mission. Forge ahead despite your family's indifference. Once they see the results in the first room you organize, they may be willing to jump in when you're ready to tackle the next one.

CHARITY BEGINS BY CLEARING OUT YOUR HOME

If you have a favorite charitable organization, call and ask if it accepts donations of used household goods, furnishings, clothing, or whatever items you no longer want or need. Some charities will even pick the items up at your home at no cost. Or look in the Yellow Pages for thrift shops; many exist to raise funds for hospitals, children's service organizations, and other nonprofit agencies. Find one you'd like to support and inquire about what kinds of merchandise it accepts.

Before your items are picked up or dropped off, make an itemized list of what you are donating. At tax time an accountant can estimate the "market value" of the items you donated (which will be much less than what you paid for the items new, unless they are antiques that have appreciated in value). The Internal Revenue Service (IRS) will also accept "market value" estimates gleaned from recent sales on eBay; visit www.ebay.com and look under recently completed auctions to see how much items like yours are worth. Also note that some nonprofit agencies provide value estimates for donated items; ask if your chosen organization has such a list when you make your donation. To keep track of your donations for tax deduction purposes, use the chart *opposite* and keep the completed form in a tax deductions file, along with the receipts furnished by the nonprofit organizations that accepted your items.

TAX-DEDUCTIBLE DONATIONS

ITEM	MARKET VALUE	DATE OF DONATION	NAME AND TAX ID# OF CHARITY THAT ACCEPTED THE ITEM

STORE YOUR STUFF

STEP 2

FIRST STEPS TO STORAGE

Wow ... You've done it! You've cleared your life and home of everything you don't want, can't use, and perhaps never needed in the first place. You've set aside items that you want to sell or donate, relocated things that belong in other parts of your house, and gathered all the stuff that has to go to the shoemaker, tailor, or repair shop. Now all you have to do is organize the things you need, use, and enjoy.

CATEGORIZE TO CONQUER

First divide your possessions by the tasks and activities for which you use them. Most rooms serve as headquarters for more than one activity; for instance your kitchen may be used for cooking and paperwork, while your bedroom may also be your in-house cinema. Separating items by function will help you organize your spaces.

Now go through each pile and combine items that you use for each task, such as all your bill-paying supplies (stamps, envelopes, and a calculator). As you make these piles, write down what is in each; this will help you choose appropriate containers. Also consider where you will use each pile of items: Where will you perform the task? What furniture or appliances do you want close at hand? For instance your makeup needs to be near a mirror, your CD collection ought to be close to the stereo, and your everyday pots and pans belong within reach of the stove.

PLAN WITH USE IN MIND

After sorting items by common functions, separate them by frequency of use. In a bathroom toothbrushes and toothpaste get daily use, while suntan lotion may only be needed seasonally. In a closet you may have running shoes for year-round jogging and dress shoes that only come out on special occasions. Throughout your home you undoubtedly have items that you use only once or twice a year: holiday ornaments, the Thanksgiving turkey platter, the CD-ROM containing your tax-preparation software, your good silverware. You may need these things, but you don't need to access them every day. It makes sense to store such items in an attic or basement, in an underbed bin, or in a cabinet above the refrigerator, with clear labels so that it's easy to find the items when you do need them. This will free up easy-access storage space for things you use all the time.

GET IN THE ZONE

In studio apartments or living spaces that serve more than one purpose, it is especially important to divide items by function and create a separate zone for each activity. Physical dividers work well: Bookcases can be half-walls, and curtains (hung from brackets on the ceiling or on opposing walls) can provide privacy and hide utilitarian areas. Folding screens also offer a good way to create separate zones in a one-room apartment; they can be stashed if you throw a party and want the entire space to be open.

Alternately create separate zones by visual means: Instead of wall-to-wall carpet or a solid expanse of wood or tile flooring, use area rugs to delineate different zones. Or paint the walls in one portion of the space one color, with a complementary color (or a patterned wallpaper) to signal a shift to another functional zone.

In the floor plan *below* furniture, folding screens, and walls divide a large basement into various activity zones. See page 88 for more on this basement makeover.

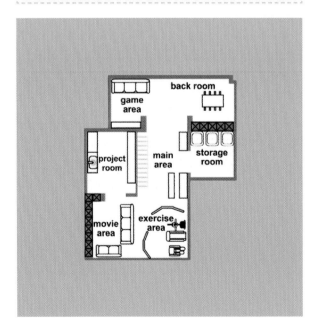

MAP YOUR MISSION

Now that you have sorted everything according to function, it's time to map out a plan. Whether you are reorganizing a small space such as a closet or overhauling an entire room, having a clear vision of what you want the space to look like will help you choose storage containers, boxes, and bins that suit your needs.

MEASURE FIRST, BUY ONCE

Along with your vision you'll need accurate measurements of your space. This will allow the purchase of containers, furnishings, and other objects that will ultimately work in the newly organized area.

First things first: Make a sketch of how you want the finished room to appear, considering all the activities you and your family do in that space. No advanced artistic skills are needed. The professional organizers on *Mission: Organization* typically use computer software to show homeowners renderings of how the finished room will look. While this can be extremely valuable, no-frills graph paper and a pencil—along with a tape measure— will get the job done, as will ordinary tracing paper and photographs of your room.

To use graph paper measure the wall heights and widths in the space you plan to tackle. Transfer the measurements onto graph paper (1 square equaling 1 square foot), noting any built-ins, windows, jogs in the wall, and so forth that you will need to take into consideration when planning your customized storage solution.

Then make templates of the furnishings you plan to include in the room, keeping in mind traffic flow and the most efficient use of space. (For instance, if your room is small, consider freestanding shelving units and wall-mounted shelves and cabinets, which keep valuable floor space free. Also consider purchasing multifunctional furnishings, such as an ottoman that has storage beneath the lid.) Next arrange the templates on the graph paper and move them around until you feel you have achieved the right balance of function and storage space. You may change your mind as you begin to purchase storage solutions; however, always keep your original plan in hand as a reminder of how big—or small—the space really is.

Photographs can also help you map your space. Enlarge each photo to fit on an 8½x11-inch sheet of paper. Lay a piece of vellum or tracing paper over the enlarged photos and use a sharp pencil to trace along any architectural features that will remain in place after the makeover. Then use colored pencils to audition various wall colors or to sketch new furnishings as shown *right*.

BUDGETING FOR THE MISSION

To avoid running out of funds midway through your mission, take some time to determine a budget. How much money do you have available to spend? How much do the containers you like cost? Does your plan involve any significant remodeling or building (such as adding a banquette with storage or installing a specialized wall system for mounting bins and baskets)?

If the cost of the chosen storage system exceeds your current budget, remember the process of sorting your stuff and eliminating the excess alone will help make your home feel less cluttered—and it can be a source of additional funds if you decide to hold a tag sale. (See pages 18 and 19 for tips.) What you make may help you finance that pricey walnut desk set, a storage armoire, or designer containers.

To save money skip the specialty stores and shop at discount chains. Or look for creative containers at other people's tag sales and secondhand stores. If money is really tight, cover old shoeboxes with gift wrap or purchase inexpensive clear disposable food containers to sort and store your things. Although they're not the most glamorous options, the difference they'll make in your quality of life will make you feel like a million bucks.

SHOPPING FOR STORAGE CONTAINERS

Don't you love the way everything looks so nice and neat in those catalogs that feature storage containers? Everything fits in the boxes perfectly, and the lids all snap on without bulges or bumps. Perhaps you imagine that if you bought a full set of those containers, your closet, home office, or garage would look as nice and neat as those photographs in the catalogs.

Not so fast. The reality is that before that glossy catalog was printed, the photographers and a staff of stylists spent countless hours choosing exactly the right contents

SMART PLANNING IDEAS Getting a clear idea of how you want your room to look and function is as easy as photographing your space and marking up the photos with potential storage solutions. See pages 174 to 184 for the crafts room and office makeover *above*.

for those containers to show them off in their best light. Of course nothing is out of place or overflowing; anything that doesn't fit in the box doesn't make it into the picture. Creating a storage system for real life is much more challenging because your system must be functional, not merely pretty. The containers have to hold all of your stuff and have to fit under your bed, on your top shelf, or on the back of your closet door.

The best way to guarantee a perfect fit is to create a written inventory of the items you want to organize and then take accurate measurements of the spaces where you plan to put whatever containers you buy (see page 29). How wide and how deep are your dresser drawers? How much space is under your bed? Also consider the style of your home and whether the containers will be tucked away or prominently displayed (see *below* for more information). With your inventory and measurements in mind, you will be able to purchase storage containers with confidence—no more feeling defeated by tidy-looking containers that refuse to fit your space!

FILE TO SUIT YOUR STYLE

Like other home furnishings, storage containers come in nearly every style imaginable, from rustic to retro-chic, traditional to trendy. Before purchasing storage containers, consider how they will look with the rest of your decor. Stainless-steel mesh containers might look great in an urban loft, but they probably won't cut it in a seaside cottage-style kitchen. If your home office is decorated in an East-meets-West style, bamboo baskets are probably a better bet than neon-color plastic boxes. For containers that complement your style, shop in the stores you frequent for other accessories. Asian import stores, for instance, offer plenty of bamboo baskets, while marine supply shops sell stand-up canvas bags that can corral magazines and toys in your beach house.

If you opt for storage containers that will be seen, you are in luck: Manufacturers have created baskets and bins that complement many decorating styles and offer attractive ways to stash your stuff. For closed storage keep furnishings with drawers, doors, and cubbies in mind. Armoires, end tables, and storage ottomans offer a convenient way to store board games, extra blankets, electronic equipment, and occasional-use items.

SIZE MATTERS

Wander through the aisles of any home improvement center and you'll see them: heavy plastic bins large enough to hold a minivan. And they're great—if you need to store a minivan. For most home uses, however, industrial-size bins are not a great choice. They can be very heavy when loaded, which makes them difficult to move when you need to retrieve a stored item or vacuum the floor beneath them. It's almost impossible to see what's in them or to access something at the bottom without emptying the whole thing—hardly an efficient way to store your stuff. Finally, these bins are often too big for their intended contents, which makes them magnets for all kinds of items that don't have other "homes." As a result you may end up with a 100-cubic-foot container that has a layer of summer sheets on the bottom and a dozen random items on top. So much for getting organized.

When are these bins a smart storage solution? When you have large yet lightweight items that are used at one time. For instance use them to stash your sweaters, blankets, or beach gear during the off-season and retrieve the items when you're ready to use them again.

AN OPEN OR SHUT CASE

While size is an important consideration when selecting storage containers, you also need to decide whether your things are best stored in open containers, on open shelves, or in sealed receptacles. Open storage works best for items that are uniform in appearance, attractive, and easy to keep neat, such as a dozen matching wash-

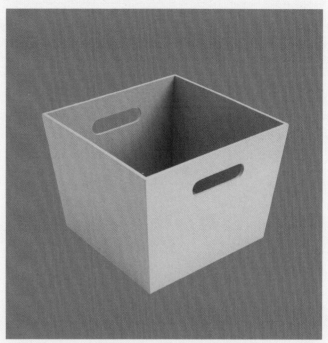

cloths in the bathroom or a set of gleaming copper pots. Anything stored in the open may become a focal point in the room, so ask yourself whether the item in question really deserves that much attention and scrutiny.

LET'S MAKE THIS PERFECTLY CLEAR—OR OPAQUE

One of the biggest decisions you'll face when you purchase storage containers is whether to buy clear plastic bins and boxes or more decorative ones made of straw, metal, wood, or other materials. The advantage of clear bins is, well, clear: You will be able to see what is inside without opening the box. That's handy if you plan to stack several boxes together—for example in a bedroom closet where you'll store shoes and sweaters or in a playroom cupboard where you'll stow toys. Another advantage is cost: No-frills clear plastic boxes are usually less expensive than decorative alternatives.

Opaque boxes usually look dressier than clear ones and help a space appear neater. That makes them a good choice for desks, tabletops, and public rooms. For example if you need a container for linen napkins in your dining room, a pretty woven Pandan box might suit your taste better than a plain plastic bin. If the item you need to store is attractive or elegant, you may want to put it in a container that is open so that the item becomes a part of the decor. Consider linen napkins again: If you have room on top of your sideboard but not inside it, you may choose to fold or roll the napkins and place them in a beautiful copper pot or an elegant ceramic bowl.

To make shopping for storage easier, use the list *opposite*. Carry it with you whenever you shop. Keep it handy even when you are not specifically looking for storage solutions; you never know when you are going to find something you can use creatively.

STORAGE CONTAINER NEEDS

ITEM TYPE OR CATEGORY	AMOUNT TO STORE	STORE IN GROUPS OR INDIVIDUALLY?	WHERE WILL THE ITEMS BE STORED?	OPEN OR CLOSED STORAGE?	CLEAR OR OPAQUE CONTAINERS?	STYLE OF CONTAINERS	DIMENSIONS OF THE AREA WHERE CONTAINERS MUST FIT

THINKING OUTSIDE THE BOX-STORE BOX

Stores and catalogs that specialize in organizational tools and supplies can be great resources for containers and filing systems, as can mass merchandisers. However, if you extend your search beyond the usual outlets, you may find some great storage options. For instance a window box from a garden center may be the perfect holder for your CD collection. Check out children's furniture stores for pieces with slots and bins typically used for toy storage; they may also work well for stacking catalogs and sorting mail. Small shelves with hooks underneath are a terrific choice for tiny bathrooms; use the hooks for robes or towels and the shelf for lotions or extra toilet paper. Food storage containers sold at supermarkets can hold hair accessories in your bedroom, hardware near your workbench, or needles and notions in your hobby room. Military surplus stores often carry duffel bags and footlockers, which may offer practical storage solutions for your basement or attic.

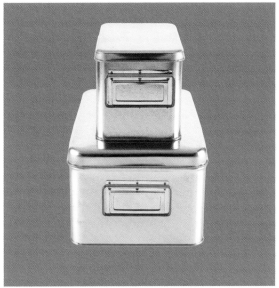

WHY DOES MY ROOM
STILL LOOK CLUTTERED?

Even after every last paper clip is stored in a container that functions well and looks great, a room may still seem disorganized. Often this is because of mismatched furniture, eclectic accessories, or copious collections. If you have sorted and stored everything and your room still looks haphazard, read on.

If your furniture is the problem, give the mismatched pieces a more uniform look. Paint all the secondhand kitchen chairs white or reupholster the flea market finds in coordinating fabrics. Group pieces that are similar in form or in scale and rearrange the furniture if necessary, reevaluating traffic flow and ensuring that the room has appropriate furnishings for all the activities that take place there. Do you have more furnishings than you need? If so eliminate some. When furnishings are cohesive and well-edited, your rooms look fresher and more organized.

If collectibles have taken over your home, consider this: Collections have more impact when they're displayed together; so instead of having one figurine near the sofa, another on the mantel, and two more in the powder room, move them all to one location. Grouping them together will make it easier to decide which ones detract from the collection; you may choose to store these items and rotate them into your display, or you could get rid of them altogether. Rotating your displays ensures that all your items get due attention; it also streamlines the look of the room and keeps the space lively and interesting. For a different look group items by color and redistribute them throughout the house (for instance, display all your pink collectibles in the living room and all the blue pieces in the kitchen).

Finally consider whether the surfaces in your room—walls, floor, ceiling—contribute to a cohesive look. Painting the walls and updating the flooring (if you can afford it) will give your room a fresh start. Choose colors that complement your furnishings and accessories—and the style you've established in the space—to pull the look together.

STEP 3
STAY
ORGANIZED

LIVING THE CLUTTER-FREE LIFE

Once your space is organized, the challenge may be to keep it organized. To meet the challenge you must prevent superfluous stuff from entering your home in the first place and develop an ongoing organization plan. For specific tips on keeping individual rooms organized, see pages 38 to 65; for a general strategy, make the following resolutions to lessen the amount of clutter that accumulates in your home.

CLEAR YOUR PLATE

First, if you receive a gift that you don't absolutely love, exchange it at the store for something you can use—or for credit to be used at a later date. Next learn to say no. Whether you're being offered your sister's cast-off sofa or the chance to chair a committee, give yourself permission to decline. Whenever you say no, you make more room in your life for an object, activity, or friendship that you would truly enjoy. Finally rein in your hobbies. If you're in the middle of knitting six sweaters or building four birdhouses, put away all but one. Resolve not to start another until you've finished every project you've begun.

DEVELOP ORGANIZED HABITS

To ensure that the things you own and cherish remain organized, schedule regular tune-ups—just as you would for your car—for each room in your home. In addition, every time you acquire something new, get rid of something old. (Buying a new pair of shoes? Toss your least favorite pair. Purchasing a new novel? Choose one book from your shelf and pass it along to a friend or your local library.) Purchase an attractive "relocate" bin for each area of your home, such as a large wicker basket or a beautiful woven tote bag. At the end of each day, spend a few minutes returning items to their proper locations. Tidy your work space or living area each time you finish using it. Wash and put away every dish after meals and check that your children's toys are picked up immediately after playtime. Leaving things lying around "just this once" is usually the beginning of organization's end. Finally discard all periodicals that are more than a week old. If you have already read it, you don't need it anymore—and if you have not yet opened it, you probably never will.

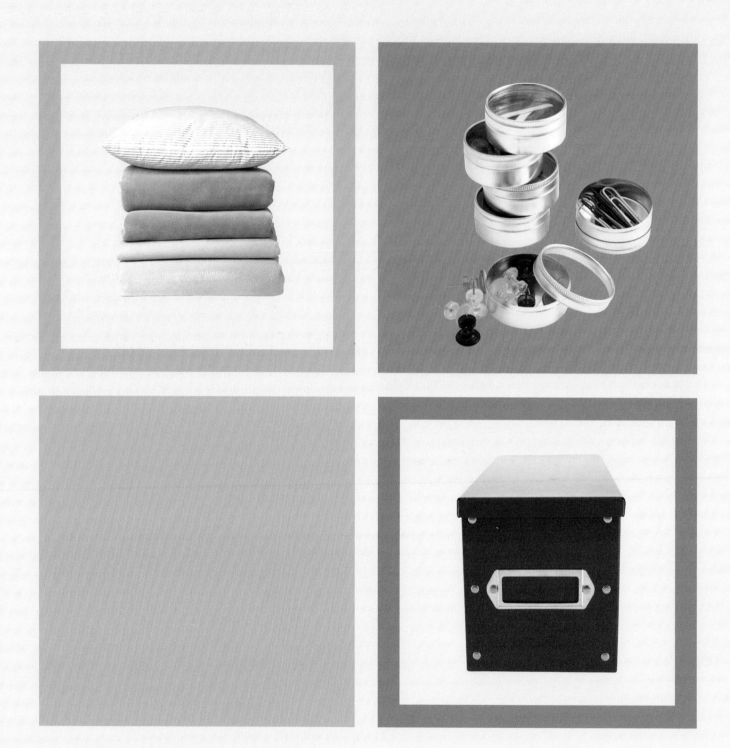

CALL IN THE PROFESSIONALS

If you're having trouble with any part of organizing your space, consider hiring a professional organizer. An organizer can teach you how to stop storing things you don't need and losing things you do need. After working with a professional organizer, you may realize that you have been shopping to fill an emotional or spiritual void. The services of an organizer will quickly pay for themselves if they help you eliminate this behavior.

First ask friends and family members for referrals; personal recommendations are the best way to find an organizer. If no one has used a professional organizer, call your local chamber of commerce and look for ads in regional magazines. Or contact the National Association of Professional Organizers for a list of professionals in your area. Visit www.napo.net or www.association-office.com/napo/referral/index.htm.

Interview several organizers over the phone. Getting organized is a personal process, and it is best to work with someone who understands and respects the way you think and the way you live. Ask each candidate how long he or she has been in business, what the fees are, and whether the charge is by the hour or the project. Also ask about the working style of each organizer and always ask for references. If your first impression is positive and the references seem enthusiastic, ask the organizer to come to your home for a free consultation. During that time he or she should be able to assess your mess, estimate how long the project will take, and tally the additional expenses you may incur (for specialty products, carpentry, and so forth). If you like what you hear, go ahead and set a date to start working.

HELP IS ON THE WAY The homeowners who appear on *Mission: Organization* enlist professional organizers to help them clear the clutter from their homes. Two boys gain a refreshed basement bedroom *top* **(see page 126), while a husband-wife team regains two rooms for home computing and crafting** *above* **(see page 174).**

RESIST THE URGE

One way to stop clutter from entering your home is to stay out of souvenir shops when you travel. Give up the practice of bringing something back from every vacation or day trip. Before you purchase anything on your travels, ask yourself if you'd buy it in a store in your own neighborhood. Carefully consider why you want a souvenir and where you will display it.

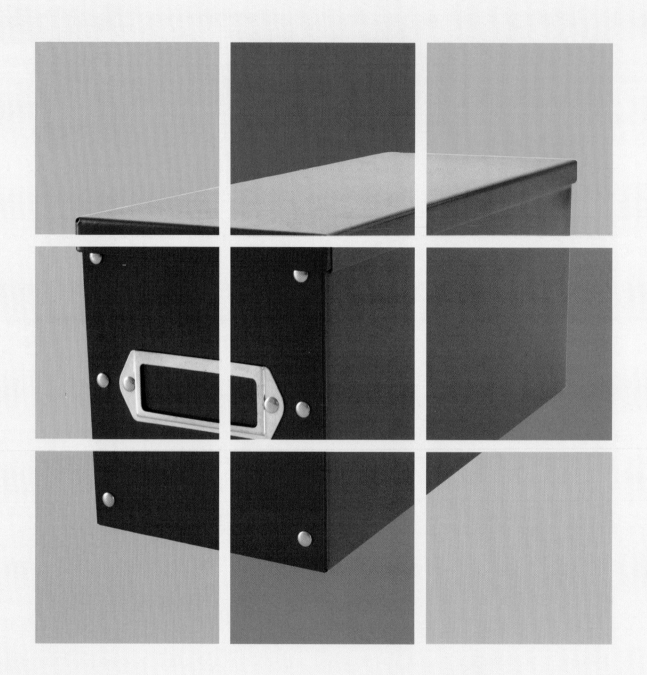

A ROOM-BY-ROOM GUIDE TO CUTTING THE CLUTTER

In the previous section you learned why it's important to rid your home—and your life—of what you don't need and don't use. You've read about a three-step process professional organizers use to clear the clutter from clients' homes and their own houses. Now it's time to put what you've learned into action! This section gives you tips and strategies to sort and store the contents of your kitchen, living room, bedroom, and more. You'll also find tricks for keeping clutter at bay after the cleaning, sorting, and storing is done. Are you ready to embark on your own Mission: Organization? If so choose your challenge and prepare for a rewarding journey.

MISSION: ORGANIZE YOUR KITCHEN

Are you planning to host a dinner party every night for the next decade? Are you a budding gourmet chef? If not you can probably get by without dozens of cookbooks, seven different pie plates, and enough spices to reopen the East India Trading Company. Organizing your kitchen—and eliminating excess utensils, gadgets, and small appliances—will make meal preparation easier and allow you to spend more quality time with your family in the heart of your home. Follow these tips for sorting and storing kitchen necessities—and read on to learn how to keep clutter under control after you complete your kitchen mission.

■ Get rid of any cookbook, gadget, or ingredient you haven't used in the past year. If you haven't found a need for it in that time, you probably never will.

Do you clip recipes from magazines? If your kitchen is suffering from your habit, toss the recipes you haven't used in a year and put your favorites in divided photo album pages that slip into a binder. To make recipes easy to find, separate them into categories (salads, desserts, etc.) and then use tabs to label the categories.

■ Toss any spices that have lost their scent; they are no longer fresh and will not offer full flavor. (In the future buy small quantities to ensure freshness and consider growing herbs on your windowsill so that you can snip the exact amount you need.)

■ If you have bulky baking equipment—such as large pans and tins—that you use once or twice a year, eliminate it. Instead use inexpensive disposable tins and resolve to throw them away after each use. You'll free up space for everyday items.

■ Breaking up is smart to do! Although many kitchen supplies and utensils are sold as coordinating sets, you are under no obligation to keep all the pieces. Retain only the items you actually use and donate the rest.

■ Are your cabinets filled with food storage containers, some of which are stained or damaged? Do you spend time searching for lids to match the containers? It's time to sort! If your containers are stained, wash them with a specialty cleaning product; if this doesn't work, throw them out. If your containers are damaged, toss them; otherwise their contents may seep out and damage something else. Finally pair every container with a matching lid. Get rid of all lids and containers that don't have a partner.

■ Scrutinize your dishes, glasses, and serving pieces. If you have miscellaneous pieces that don't coordinate, get rid of them. Also sort your plastic cups and other throwaways: How many sports squeeze bottles do you really need?

CLUTTER-FREE COUNTERTOPS
Keeping countertops orderly can be difficult. Divide the contents of your countertops into different categories: items you use daily, items you use weekly, and items you use only once in a while. Keep the daily-use utensils and appliances—such as the coffeemaker and toaster—on the countertop and store the weekly-use items in an easy-to-reach spot. Consider whether you have room in your kitchen for seasonal or holiday-specific items. For example if you bake only for holiday celebrations, your mixer, cookie sheets, and related supplies could be stored in an out-of-the-way place.

STORE IT

■ After you've weeded out the unnecessary elements in your kitchen, organize the "keepers" for maximum efficiency. Group frequently used items together—mixing bowls near measuring cups and the pasta pot near the strainer—and store them near the appropriate appliance (for instance put pots and pans near the range).

■ Instead of bending over and sorting through a whole cabinet of pots every time you want to make a bowl of soup, invest in a wall- or ceiling-hung pot rack. A rack makes it easier to access your pots and pans and frees up cabinet space. Position the rack carefully to avoid bumping your head.

■ Many cabinet shelves can be raised and lowered by inserting shelf pegs into alternate predrilled holes in the cabinet interior. Adjust shelf heights to better accommodate dishes, glasses, and canned goods. Incorporating freestanding metal or plastic shelf units can double the amount of stacking space on your shelves.

■ If you are remodeling or building a kitchen, consider deep drawers instead of cabinets for undercounter storage. Drawers allow you to view their contents more easily than shelves do. If you don't plan to remodel your existing kitchen, stretch your storage space—and give yourself easy access to cabinet contents—by retrofitting cabinets with drawers.

■ Racks that allow you to store plates on their sides instead of in a stack make it easier to reach plates when you need them. Rack storage also reduces the chance of breakage.

■ Attach a metal or plastic grid to a wall and hang items on S hooks. Use wall-hung magnetic knife racks to keep cutting implements sharp and at hand. *Safety note: Ensure that knives and other sharp objects are placed where children cannot reach them.*

■ Stepped shelf expanders allow you to see what's behind the front row of food in your cupboard. Using these makes it much easier to prepare your grocery list.

■ Silverware organizers can hold more than flatware. Place one or two in your "junk drawer" (yes, even the most organized households probably have one) to separate scissors and rubber bands from twist ties and pocket change.

■ If you need extra storage space, consider space-saving furniture options. Built-in banquettes and freestanding benches that have hinged tops offer excellent storage for infrequently used items, such as party platters and specialty linens.

■ If you have a collection of cookie cutters that you use only once or twice a year, let them serve as a decorative accent throughout the year. Hang them on brads above a window or doorway. When you are ready to use them for holiday baking, wash them and start cutting!

■ Kitchens with open shelves often look contemporary; however, they aren't practical for everyone. If you love the look of open cabinets but know the reality of grease splatters, consider glass-fronted cabinets. They'll keep the contents clean and still let you see what's inside.

■ If your kitchen also serves as a home office, create a work zone as far from your food prep and cooking areas as possible. Besides preventing spaghetti sauce splatters on your documents, you'll reduce the chance of fire caused by flying paperwork. Also keep some distance between your work space and your eating surface; that way your papers can lie undisturbed during mealtimes, and your project will move forward faster with fewer interruptions.

■ Freestanding islands and carts offer storage space and a work surface. To decide whether you have room for one, cut a piece of kraft paper to the same dimensions as the unit you plan to buy; then put the template on the floor where you want the unit to stand. Observe how you and your family maneuver around the template. Does it impede traffic? Adjust the size of the template until you find the right fit for your space. If you can't find a size that works, consider wall-hung grids, pot racks, or carts and racks that hug the wall to conserve floor space.

STAY ORGANIZED

■ Unless you prepare gourmet meals or entertain frequently, avoid costly specialty cooking or baking equipment that will eat up cabinet and drawer space. Many delicious meals have been prepared without a larding needle!

■ To prevent cooking magazines from accumulating, cancel your subscriptions and instead download recipes off the websites of your favorite magazines. Clip and store your favorite recipes from the magazines you have and toss the rest.

■ Whenever you store leftovers, label the containers with the contents and date. Do the same for bulk purchases: Storing cereals, flour, and other bulk items in airtight containers ensures your purchases will stay fresh longer; labels eliminate the need for guessing at the contents or the age of the stored goods.

■ If you're cooking something that requires an exotic or rarely used ingredient, make extra batches of the dish to use up the ingredient. Then you won't waste storage space on half-full bottles and containers. Freeze the meals in clearly labeled containers and reheat for dinners on the run.

■ If you already have half-full bottles or boxes on your shelves, visit the myriad cooking websites where you can type in the name of a food you have on hand and find a recipe that will help you use it. These sites are also a great place to find recipes, reducing the need for dozens of cookbooks.

■ Resist all those cute refrigerator magnets— or at least limit your display to a few at a time and rotate them regularly. They make even the most organized kitchen look cluttered.

@ FOR MORE IDEAS ON ORGANIZING YOUR KITCHEN, VISIT WWW.HGTV.COM/ORGANIZED.

MISSION: ORGANIZE YOUR BATHROOM

I s your vanity covered with tubes, bottles, and containers? Are your cabinets overflowing with towels, extra shampoo bottles, bars of soap, makeup, and cleaning supplies? Typically bathrooms have limited space, and many people have a tendency to keep medicines and hygiene-related items for too long. The inevitable result is clutter. Use these ideas for cleaning out what you don't need, storing the essentials, and keeping your bath in good order. Whether you want an invigorating place to start your day or relaxing haven after a long day of work, organizing can make your dream bath a reality.

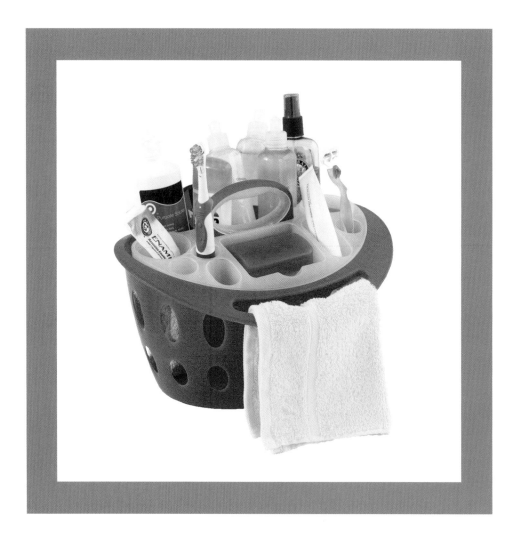

SORT IT

■ How many shampoos, styling products, and shower gels do you really need? If you have dozens of partially used bottles, pitch those you don't intend to finish. If you have several bottles of the same product, combine them. As an alternative, transfer the contents to small plastic bottles and use them for travel.

■ Get rid of expired medicines. Over time their chemical makeup changes, rendering them less effective. Call your local pharmacy for tips on proper disposal of both liquids and tablets to keep pets, children, and the environment safe. To keep moisture from ruining medicines, consider removing them from the bathroom altogether.

■ Are you planning to crimp your hair? Do you still need a flattening iron? Hair-related equipment can take up considerable space, so toss or donate any equipment items you no longer use.

■ Look at every makeup product you have: Lipstick, powder, mascara, and other common products typically have a shelf life of only six months, so throw away anything older than that. If you have sunscreen that's more than two years old, toss it.

■ Do you have old towels that are thinning, stained, or frayed? If so toss them; or cut them and use the rags for washing the car or the floor. Another great idea: Donate them to a local animal shelter.

■ If you have a bath or cleaning product you don't like, dispose of it. You are unlikely to change your mind about its scent or performance.

LABELS MAKE THE DIFFERENCE Storing items in clear containers makes it easy to see what's inside. Affixing a label to the container or shelf edge takes away any guesswork when you're searching for or returning an item. See page 154 for more on this bathroom.

MISSION: BATH

See page 154 for a bath that doubles as a dressing room—and combines lots of tricks to keep cleaning supplies, makeup, and more neat and organized.

STORE IT

■ Always keep safety in mind when storing bath-room-related products, including cosmetics, medicines, and cleaning supplies. Ensure they are stored or contained where curious children and pets can't reach them.

■ If your bath doesn't have a medicine cabinet and you are short on floor space, look for slim cabinets (available at home centers and mass merchandisers) that easily install above the toilet. If you have enough floor space, consider a freestanding rack or shelf for storing rolled hand towels, extra toilet tissue, and kids' bath toys; coordinated baskets and bins will keep it tidy.

■ If your bath is large enough to accommodate it, consider a storage bench. Cover the top with terry cloth or another moisture-loving fabric for post-bath seating; under the lid stow extra towels, toilet tissue, or other bulky items.

■ While the packaging of many bath-related products is attractive, it may not be uniform. To bring visual order to a space, purchase inexpensive matching glass or plastic bottles and fill them with your favorite shampoos, lotions, and soaps. Use a label that coordinates with your decor to pull the look together.

■ Use inexpensive drawer dividers—including silverware trays—to separate makeup, hair accessories, and medical supplies within a drawer.

■ Look for shower curtains that have pockets for bottles, toys, and other bath-related items. These pockets keep items off narrow tub ledges, which makes cleaning easier. Also consider baskets and bins with suction cups that attach to the shower wall. A shower caddy can also keep small items contained.

■ Lightweight mesh bags offer a great way to store bath-time toys; hang one from the shower nozzle or water spout for easy access.

■ Install hooks or rods to hang towels, pajamas, and robes with ease. Because these items can be heavy, install the hardware directly into a wall stud. Or use over-the-door towel racks and hooks to keep these items handy yet out of the way.

■ Store like items together to make them easier to find. For undersink storage purchase clear plastic bins of uniform size and stash all your extra bar soap, makeup, and toothbrushes. Clearly label the bins and stack them to maximize space.

■ Clear the countertops. Keep out a few daily-use items, such as toothbrushes and facial lotion; store the rest, including cosmetics and razors, in drawers or cabinets. Keep all countertop supplies in attractive containers—cotton swabs and balls in decorative boxes, mouthwash in a glass bottle.

■ If you have a pedestal sink, consider adding a fabric skirt. Measure a piece of fabric wide enough to go around your sink and long enough to reach the floor; then add ½ inch on each side. Cut out the fabric and use ½-inch-wide fusible hem tape to fuse the raw edges to the back of the skirt. Attach the skirt with hook-and-loop tape and use it to conceal bins and baskets filled with toilet tissue and other essentials you may not want to display.

■ Customize your existing cabinets and drawers with specialty pullout bins and lazy Susans. These products are widely available at home centers and can be installed in a snap. Also look for tilt-out panels that fit on the front of the vanity. They're handy for storing slim items such as toothbrushes and curling irons.

STAY ORGANIZED

■ Select bath- and hygiene-related products that you and your mate can share to reduce excess bottles, containers, and cans.

■ Everyone loves a bargain—and getting free cosmetic samples may seem like a great way to test new products. However, this is a sure way to clutter your cabinets and drawers. Keep only the samples you really want and either give the others to family or friends or throw them away. Better yet, leave the samples at the store for someone else to enjoy.

■ Bath products, candles, and the like have become increasingly popular gifts for special occasions. You may end up with more than you can use. Instead of dutifully storing these away, donate them to nonprofit shelters for people in need. Then, unless you actually need more, discourage gift-givers from purchasing such items for you.

@ FOR MORE IDEAS ON ORGANIZING YOUR BATHROOM, VISIT WWW.HGTV.COM/ORGANIZED.

MISSION: ORGANIZE YOUR BEDROOM

Do you use your bedroom for sleeping only—or does it serve as headquarters for watching TV, sorting laundry, checking e-mails, and exercising? Either way an organized bedroom will help your daily life run more smoothly and it will ensure restful nights as well. Because clothes are the biggest clutter culprit in bedrooms, this section is devoted to corralling your clothing and related items. If you have a television or stereo in your bedroom, see pages 59 and 60 for ideas on sorting and storing music and movies. For strategies to organize a work space, see pages 55 to 57.

SORT IT

To tame your wardrobe keep only the clothes that suit your current lifestyle. If you haven't played tennis since 1987, give up those tennis whites. And be honest about the size of your clothing; if you haven't worn a particular size since high school, get rid of any items in that size.

Toss clothing that's uncomfortable. If it pulls, binds, or rides up, get rid of it. Life is too short to walk in tight shoes!

Empty all your drawers and throw away orphaned socks, hosiery that is stretched out or has runs and snags, and ill-fitting undergarments.

Sort the clothes you are keeping by season. Only in-season clothes need to be at hand; the rest can be stored at the back of your closet or in underbed containers.

SMART SOLUTIONS After a major clear-out and reorganization, this small bedroom allows the occupant to sleep, work on the computer, and hang out with friends with ease. See page 136 for more on this space.

STORE IT

Do you and your mate keep your clothes in separate dressers? If you have one piece with small drawers and one with large drawers, it may make more sense for you both to store undergarments and T-shirts in the chest with small drawers; then put all the bulky sweaters in the larger, deeper drawers.

If space is tight, install coat hooks on the back wall of your closet; hang out-of-season clothes flat against the wall.

To prevent sweaters and knits from stretching in the shoulders, fold and store them on shelves, not hangers. If shelf space is limited, store your sweaters flat or fold them in half and hang them over a padded hanger.

If your closet has sliding doors, replace them with bifold doors or floor-length curtains that open completely. Then you'll be able to see your entire wardrobe at a glance and choose an outfit with ease. No more fighting with sliding doors that have come off their tracks.

MISSION: BEDROOM

See page 136 for a bedroom that goes from girly-girly to grown-up with some savvy storage solutions, some fresh paint, and a new layout. To see a guest room dug out of a disorganized attic, turn to page 166.

■ In the closet take advantage of the floor space under your short hanging items. Purchase clear containers and stash out-of-season sweaters and shoes under your skirts or blouses.

■ If you store sweaters or T-shirts on a top shelf, use vertical shelf dividers to keep the stacks from tumbling into one another.

■ Most closets have plenty of space above the hanging bar. If you don't already have shelves up there, consider installing some. Better yet, take a careful inventory of what you need to store there and order compartmentalized cubbies that will keep items separate and easy to grab.

■ Are moths a problem where you reside? If so use cedar hangers or buy cedar blocks to keep the pests at bay.

■ Do you have a lot of costume jewelry? Fishing tackle boxes are a great way to sort earrings and pins, while pegboard will prevent necklaces from becoming tangled. Hide the board on the inside of the closet, or mount it on a wall to show off a prized collection.

■ If you watch television in your bedroom, consider splurging on a wall-mounted TV. If the TV is currently in an armoire, that space will be available for additional clothes storage. If the TV has been sitting on your dresser, removing it will make the entire room look less cluttered.

■ Blanket chests can store lots of other things. Use them for out-of-season clothes, bedding, towels, or videos and CDs.

■ Stack new or vintage hatboxes in the "dead space" on top of an armoire or on a deep wall-hung corner shelf. Fill the boxes with seldom-used hosiery, lingerie, and other small, lightweight items.

■ Build or purchase a headboard with shelves or compartments. Use the cubbies to store nighttime reading, favorite keepsakes, or pretty lidded baskets for stashing scarves or costume jewelry.

■ Think vertical rather than horizontal, especially in a small room. For instance an armoire can store more clothes than a long dresser, and the armoire requires less floor space. A tall, narrow lingerie chest offers more storage per square inch of floor space than a short, squat dresser.

■ Consider using a low bookcase as a night table. The top shelf can hold your lamp, telephone, and alarm clock, while the lower shelves can store opaque boxes filled with reading material, jewelry, or lotions.

■ If your dresser top is cluttered with keepsakes and photos, store some and rotate the display monthly or seasonally.

■ Invest in drawer dividers to keep socks, hosiery, and undergarments organized.

■ It works for kids, and it will work for you: Every night before you turn in, choose your outfit for the next day. This will help you avoid those last-minute wardrobe crises that usually result in all your clothing lying in a tangled heap on the floor.

■ Live by this rule: When you buy something new, get rid of something old—yes, shoes and clothing articles included. This keeps your wardrobe fresh and prevents your closet and drawers from becoming overloaded.

■ Resist the urge to purchase sale items unless you really need and love them. Jeans for $5 are only a great buy if they fit well and you need them; otherwise they really aren't a bargain.

■ Keep things visible. Use clear shoe bags instead of patterned ones. If you prefer your shoes in boxes, invest in clear acrylic containers or attach snapshots of your shoes to the outside of the box for quick identification. Consider clear boxes for your sweaters and T-shirts too.

■ Purchase a laundry basket for each member of your family. Sort the laundry into the baskets as you fold it and you'll avoid that massive pile of household laundry at the end of your bed.

STORAGE HIDEAWAYS

Concealing large items in a bedroom may seem like a difficult task. However, a folding screen or a bed skirt may help solve some of your storage problems.

■ Buy or make a folding screen and place it in a corner of the room. It can hide your hamper, conceal a separate area for exercise or computer work, or create a private reading nook. Affix hooks to the back and store small items such as bags, belts, and costume jewelry.

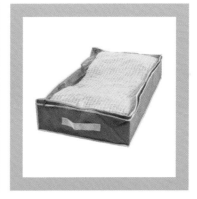

■ Underbed bins offer a great place for out-of-season clothes, special-occasion bags and shoes, or a change of bed linens. If your bed can accommodate a dust ruffle, get one—it will conceal the bins.

@ FOR MORE IDEAS ON ORGANIZING YOUR CLOSETS, VISIT WWW.HGTV.COM/ORGANIZED.

HGTV MISSION: ORGANIZATION **49**

MISSION: ORGANIZE YOUR KIDS' ROOMS AND PLAYROOMS

Unless you want to become your children's full-time maid, you cannot keep them entirely organized. However, it is possible to help them keep chaos to a minimum by themselves. Use these clever tricks and sneaky strategies to prevent your children's bedroom or play space from caving in to clutter.

SORT IT

■ Weed out clothes that are too small and either donate them or give them to friends or family. It's OK to hold on to special, gently worn clothing for a younger sibling. Clearly label the container that holds the items and store it where the contents will not be damaged by the elements.

■ Check that all toys have their requisite pieces. Set aside those that are incomplete and give yourself two weeks to find the missing pieces. If you don't find the necessary pieces and parts by the deadline, toss the toy in the trash. Also gauge the condition of stuffed toys and dolls. If they are stained or worn and if their eyes are missing, throw them out.

■ If you can't bring yourself to throw away your child's art projects, ask him or her which three are most important. Frame those and turn the rest into gift wrap or birthday cards. Laminate large paintings to make place mats and give them as gifts.

■ If your children are too far apart in age (or interests) to share toys, separate their things into individual piles. Inventory them separately and choose storage that suits each child's age and height.

FIT FOR KIDS This play space *top* (see page 118) is carved out of a pass-through. Convertible furnishings and fun colors make the bedroom *above* (see page 126) a perfect fit for two brothers.

MISSION: KIDS' SPACES

For a colorful basement bedroom shared by two young boys, see page 126. If you are looking for smart play-space solutions, see the playroom-laundry area on page 118.

If you are creating a nursery, purchase furnishings and storage solutions that can make the transition from tiny baby clothing to toddler clothing with ease.

Once you have narrowed your storage choices to a few options, allow your kids to make the final choice. Feeling involved in the process will help motivate them to keep things organized.

Decide which books and toys will go in your child's room and which will reside in the family room or playroom. Place an attractive "relocate" basket in each space for proper redistribution of stuff at the end of each day. Choose a medium-weight or lightweight basket that a child can easily carry.

If your children have beautiful picture books they have practically memorized, carefully remove the pages and frame favorite illustrations. Discarding or recycling the rest of the book makes room for new volumes. The inexpensive and instant art can be tossed and replaced with new illustrations as your children's tastes change.

Arrange storage containers so your kids can reach them and easily lift them if necessary. Install hooks or cubbies where they can put their toys, book bags, coats, and mittens without your assistance.

For children's bookcases and dressers, think long and low rather than high and narrow. This will allow your child to reach all of his or her books—and the lower furniture is to the ground, the less likely it is to tip over. *Safety note: If floor space is limited and you need to use tall bookcases, anchor them to the wall.*

For the best toy storage, choose smaller individual boxes instead of a giant toy chest. Clear containers are best, because they allow your child to see what is inside without opening the lids. If you must use opaque containers, staple a photo of the contents to the back of the box. If your children are old enough to read, label their toy boxes with words.

HEADACHE PREVENTION

If your kids always fight over a particular toy, get rid of it. It's important to teach children how to share; however, peace and quiet is equally important.

■ Captain's beds have drawers beneath the mattress, providing convenient storage for large or heavy toys that can't be safely stored higher up. The drawers are also handy for seldom-worn clothing like snow pants.

■ In closets utilize the space beneath hung clothing. Consider building cubbies for sweaters and pants. Or install a bar at lower-than-standard height so your child can reach it; then install shelves above for out-of-season clothing.

■ Clear vinyl shoe bags are great organizers for the inside of closet doors. In kids' rooms put hair accessories, rolled-up socks, or undergarments in the lower pockets and out-of-season items in the upper portions. Similarly use clear organizers for mittens and scarves in your front hall closet, putting the kids' stuff on lower shelves and the adult accessories higher up.

■ Store out-of-season clothes out of your toddler's view and reach; this will help eliminate power struggles about wearing shorts on cold winter mornings.

STAY ORGANIZED

■ Once you have organized your child's room or playroom, take "after" pictures that show where everything belongs. Post the photos where your child can see them. In theory this will limit the amount of adult assistance required at cleanup time.

■ Choosing outfits the night before eliminates morning commotion. To help your child with clothing selection, put clean laundry into drawers by outfit rather than clothing type; then your child can see what clothes go well together.

■ Create a homework zone in your child's room and discourage the use of the kitchen table for school assignments. Work done in the kitchen is invariably disrupted by snacks or suppertime. If your kids must work in the kitchen, set up a designated space—not your cooking prep counters—for them to stow notebooks and school supplies when not in use.

■ If your child becomes bored with his or her books, toys, or videos, resist the urge to buy more. Instead organize a swap with families who have children the same age. Your kids will get a bunch of brand new toys without needing any more storage space (and without your spending any money).

@ FOR MORE IDEAS ON GETTING THE WHOLE FAMILY ORGANIZED, VISIT WWW.HGTV.COM/ORGANIZED.

HGTV MISSION: ORGANIZATION **53**

MISSION: ORGANIZE YOUR HOME OFFICE

Whether you work from home full time, bring work home from the office occasionally, or restrict your at-home work to paying bills, your home office has to accommodate multiple tasks. Your office may be a little niche in the kitchen or bedroom or an entire room; either way it is a potential clutter magnet. Piles of paperwork, stacks of computer disks and CDs, and vast amounts of small, oddly shaped supplies seem to multiply on their own. Follow these strategies to transform a chaotic office into a neat and tidy work zone.

SORT IT

■ If more than one person uses your home office, sort papers by user first; then sort by type and importance. Create a separate file drawer for each person if possible; or at the very least, assign a certain folder color for each user.

■ Do you have a big jar or drawer full of pens and pencils? How many of them leak or don't work at all? Toss all the ones that don't write smoothly and cleanly. Throw out scissors that don't cut neatly, pencil erasers that crumble, rubber bands that have lost their elasticity, and correction fluid that is no longer fluid.

■ If you use your office for hobbies such as scrapbooking, quilting, sewing, or building model airplanes—sort your supplies by activity. Eliminate duplicate supplies and identify broken or worn-out materials. Dull needles and dried-up paint have no use; they merely take up space.

■ Determine which books you really need to store on your shelves. If you haven't opened a biology text since college—and your career or hobbies aren't related to the science—get rid of it.

HOLD IT; DON'T THROW IT!
Some household paperwork must be kept in storage even if you have not looked at it in more than a year. Your old tax records will probably never see the light of day. However, if the Internal Revenue Service (IRS) does call, you will likely need to furnish tax returns from the past three years.

MISSION: HOME OFFICES
For an office that perfectly meets the needs of three people, see page 96. Go to page 174 for two hobby rooms that combine great storage solutions with vibrant color and pattern.

STORE IT

■ Stash all your desk supplies—staples, paper clips, rubber bands—in pint-size containers, such as teacups, plastic cubes, or bowls. Keep scissors and staplers on your desk only if you use them frequently; otherwise dedicate a drawer or box to these bulky items to keep your desk top clear.

■ If your home office is a separate room, you have the luxury of keeping files out in the open while a project is in progress. A large desk or table with standing files at eye level will help you keep track of work in progress; metal or even plastic filing cabinets can hold records of completed projects.

■ If your office space is best suited to bookcases and filing cabinets, purchase a series of coordinating binders and a three-hole punch. Store all your documents in the binders; keep them organized with the help of dividers, tabs, and pockets.

■ Use large hanging files for broad categories—for example "Taxes." Then create file folders for narrow topics within each category—in this case donations, business expenses, and deductions. Use tabs to delineate which file holds what paperwork.

■ If your home office is in your bedroom or the living room, store rarely needed files in specially fitted wood or wicker boxes, in a trunk/coffee table with standing file dividers tucked inside, or in a filing cabinet that's draped with an attractive cloth to serve as an accent table.

■ File papers instead of piling them. Receipts and other important documents get lost in piles. Storing files vertically makes them easier to see, find, and refile.

■ File frequently used papers in your most accessible cabinets and put "just in case papers" in banker's boxes or other sturdy containers. *Note: Because they are not moisture-proof, banker's boxes cannot be stored in basements or garages. Use portable plastic file boxes for storage in moisture-prone areas.*

■ Keep a folder for the manuals and warranty cards that came with all the appliances that you buy. When something breaks you will have the information you need at your fingertips (including how to find an authorized repair center).

IT'S A WRAP

To avoid storing a year's worth of greeting cards for every possible occasion, buy one box of beautiful blank cards and customize them with the appropriate wishes. Instead of purchasing one roll of gift wrap for bridals howers, another for graduation, and more for child and grown-up birthdays, Christmas, and Hanukkah, buy solid-color paper that will appeal to anyone (for example, turquoise, red, or yellow). Then customize with stickers or special ribbon. Store all your gift-wrapping supplies in a slim underbed container or a handy caddy that hangs on the back of a closet door.

STAY ORGANIZED

■ Storing crafts and hobby supplies in clear containers keeps them conveniently in view—perfect for identification as well as inspiration.

■ Resolve not to start any crafts projects until you've finished the one you're currently working on. Throw out unfinished projects if you haven't touched them in the last six months.

■ Avoid the temptation to print out every e-mail and computer file; let the computer memory do its job. Make hard copies only if a document is vitally important and losing it in a computer crash would be disastrous. If you are unsure, copy files onto floppy disks or CDs as a backup.

■ The best place to stem the tide of papers that wants to flood your house is right at the mailbox, where most paper clutter originates. Keep a trash can at the door where you enter with the mail and toss junk mail right away, without even bringing it near your desk.

■ If you use a bulletin board in your office, make a point to move (and throw out, if necessary) every piece of paper every week. Otherwise your eye will grow accustomed to what is posted, and important reminders will virtually fade into the walls.

■ Cancel your catalog subscriptions and visit your favorite merchants online instead. Consider discontinuing your newspaper too; even local news is now available online.

■ Be conservative about how many photographs and collectibles you display on your desk or shelves.

■ If two or more adults live in your household, avoid duplication of efforts—and misplaced paperwork—by assigning each category of paperwork to one and only one individual. For instance one person can complete school and camp forms, and the other can handle health insurance forms and doctor bills. This will reduce the likelihood of important paperwork being forgotten.

■ To reduce paperwork, go paperless! Store addresses and important dates in a wireless device and use computer programs to pay bills. To be safe create a backup disk or CD in case of a crash.

■ Provide separate in-boxes for everyone in your household. Sort your own mail into three piles: bills to pay, invitations or solicitations to respond to, and things to read. Open the bills as soon as you receive them, discarding any bill stuffers. If it's financially feasible, do all your bill paying in one weekly session. Respond to invitations and requests for donations once a week. When you accept an invitation, record the details in your daily planner or calendar and discard the loose invitation itself.

@ FOR MORE IDEAS ON ORGANIZING YOUR HOME OFFICE, VISIT WWW.HGTV.COM/ORGANIZED.

HGTV MISSION: ORGANIZATION **57**

MISSION: ORGANIZE YOUR LIVING ROOM

O nce upon a time, the living room was a formal space, saved for special company and kept as clean and clutter-free as a luxury hotel lobby. However, living rooms of this kind are generally a thing of the past. Most living rooms now do double or triple duty as family rooms, playrooms, and home offices. Of course with increased activity comes a greater probability of clutter. The tips in this section will help you curb clutter in your living room, whether it's a multipurpose place or a little-used space for entertaining.

SORT IT

■ If you have CDs you haven't listened to in more than a year, get rid of them. Or put them in the car and see if you are tempted to listen to them there. If not donate or trade them.

■ Evaluate the movies you haven't watched in a while. Do you really think you'll watch them again? If so will you watch them enough times to justify the space they take up? If not donate them to your local library.

■ If your home lacks a formal entryway, your living room may be a catchall for the mail, newspapers, your kids' homework, and everything else that makes its way through the front door. If this is the case, designate one corner of the room to serve as your "entry hall." Place a console table there to hold keys, mail, and your cell phone. Purchase a coat tree that will keep outerwear off the floor and off the backs of chairs.

■ Family photographs can add a warm, homey feeling to any space. However, if you add a picture to the display every time you develop a roll of film, the space will soon become cluttered. Change the pictures on display periodically and place them in coordinating frames to avoid a haphazard look.

■ Do you still have every knickknack you ever purchased on an impulse? If you don't still love it, get rid of it. Then if you still have a lot, showcase only a few pieces at a time on a tabletop, mantel, or shelf. Change the display regularly to keep your space looking fresh.

LIVING IT UP Replacing furniture better suited to a college dorm and corralling clutter—namely paperwork and work-related hardware—gives this living room a fresh start. Curtains keep the living area separate from an office and dining table that share the space. See page 70 for more on this room.

MISSION: LIVING ROOMS

For a multipurpose space that combines living quarters with a dining area and an office, see page 70. See page 146 for a studio apartment that has it all—a living room, an office, and a bedroom.

■ If your television and stereo equipment are making your living room look like the high school audiovisual room, consider a media armoire. Available in every style and size imaginable, such armoires offer a convenient way to contain equipment and wires, and if you purchase a unit with doors, you have the option to conceal everything whenever you wish.

■ Thousands of CD and movie containers are on the market. Select one that has enough room for all the recordings you plan to keep plus a limited amount of extra space for new additions to the collection.

■ Instead of cluttering your coffee table with multiple remote controls, a TV viewing guide, and the magazine you are reading, look for a coffee table with a spacious drawer or two or purchase an attractive tabletop caddy. Or use a trunk or a storage ottoman as a coffee table.

■ If your living room also serves as a home office, buy attractive file boxes (such as wicker, wood, or leather ones) and use them as end tables. Put a pair in front of the sofa to serve as a coffee table.

■ If your living room often serves as a playroom, divide the space into kid and adult zones. A bookcase can act as a divider and provide some storage; a folding screen will also serve the purpose. If a structure like this cuts off too much light, consider hanging a curtain rod from the ceiling, with draperies that pull to the sides. When formal company is expected, draw the draperies and make your children's toys disappear. This strategy can also hide an in-room office or exercise space.

■ Buy an attractive basket or a rack for your magazines and newspapers. Empty it every recycling day to prevent overflow.

■ If you have a large collection of art books, put a neat stack next to your sofa or favorite reading chair. Besides freeing up space on your bookshelves, you'll have a great place to set a beverage tray, a lamp, or framed photographs.

■ Look low for storage opportunities: If your sofa or chair is tall enough—and has a skirt to conceal what's below—consider using the space beneath to stow flat boxes filled with board and card games, lightweight blankets, and other slim items.

SMART SOLUTIONS FOR BOOK LOVERS

If you have a lot of books, it may pay to custom-build shelves. This will allow you to use every available inch rather than having to settle for multiples of standard bookcase width. If you go this route, ask the builder to make the shelves no deeper than your deepest books (to save on floor space) and to build them all the way up to the ceiling. Or have a series of low cubbies installed around the perimeter of the room; cover them with cushions or pillows for additional seating.

STAY ORGANIZED

■ If you find that the home office in your living room or family room dominates the whole space, hide the desk behind a folding screen. Having a set boundary will help you keep your papers from migrating.

■ Instead of buying videos and CDs, borrow them from the public library. It's free, and the selection is excellent. If you find one you really like, purchase your own copy and continue checking out freebies from the library.

■ To prevent your keepsakes and collections from taking over your home, narrow your focus: Collecting every paperweight you ever see will leave your living room looking like a flea market. Instead choose one color, shape, style, or manufacturer and limit yourself to that category. Display the items in a group on a mantel, shelf, or tabletop. Consider grouping smaller items in shadow boxes or display cases hung on the wall.

■ If you rarely or never use your fireplace, leave firewood out of the living room. If the urge to gather around the hearth strikes suddenly, pick up some logs at the supermarket.

■ Remove holiday and birthday cards from the mantel two weeks after the event. If you and your children love the motifs, recycle the cards into collage materials.

■ Provide your child with a designated "relocate" bin in the living room so that any toys and books that make their way into the space can easily be taken back to a bedroom or playroom at the end of the play session.

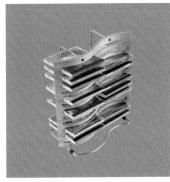

@ FOR MORE IDEAS ON ORGANIZING YOUR LIVING AND FAMILY ROOMS, VISIT WWW.HGTV.COM/ORGANIZED.

MISSION: ORGANIZE YOUR GARAGE, BASEMENT, AND ATTIC

It's where you store your special holiday dishes, out-of-season outerwear, and athletic gear. It's home to the things you haven't gotten around to throwing out, the moving boxes you still haven't unpacked, and the broken chair that needs fixing. No wonder your basement, garage, or attic is such a mess! The good news is that a lot of the things stashed there can probably be tossed. Then, with a little creative storage, you will actually be able to locate the items that you really do need to keep. Use the ideas in this section to clear out, clean up, and store like a pro.

SORT IT

▨ If you have lived in your house for more than a year and have moving-day boxes you haven't gotten around to unpacking, throw them out without even opening them. Obviously you do not need their contents.

▨ Carefully separate the items you actually use, such as tools or automotive supplies, from the items you only store. Sort the items you use by category; evaluate what you have and eliminate multiples.

▨ Take note of any chemicals or tools that could be dangerous to children or pets. When you shop for storage solutions, keep child and animal safety in mind.

▨ Throw away the TV that needs a new knob and the old vacuum cleaner that coughs up dust. If you need the appliance, you've probably replaced it by now; if you haven't replaced it, either do so or live without it.

▨ Avoid the temptation to keep broken parts after you fix something or to store leftover screws or other small items after assembling a toy chest or other furnishings. Unless you're living on a deserted island, these items are not valuable enough to store.

▨ If you have a pile of scrap lumber, chances are it could use a little whittling down. Save the largest pieces and a few of the tiny ones. Small wood blocks rarely come in handy for anything.

MISSION: GARAGES, BASEMENTS, AND ATTICS

For a garage that stores sports equipment and more for a family on the go, see page 108. If your garage is overrun with clutter—from gardening supplies to seasonal furniture—look at the garage on page 80 for some creative solutions. Looking for ways to transform a basement into a space where you can work, play, and exercise? See page 88 for great ideas.

PROPER DISPOSAL

Get rid of leftover paint. If you ever need more of a color, a few bucks will buy you a quart, which will be enough for minor touch-ups. Open any varnishes and finishes you have accumulated. If the color or texture has changed over time, toss the materials. Latex, or water-base, materials can be thrown away in your regular trash if you open the can and allow the contents to dry out. However, if the materials are alkyd, or oil-base, you must dispose of them at a toxic-waste center.

STORE IT

■ If you choose not to park your car in your garage, or if your basement or attic space will only be used for storage, make the most of the space by installing shelves against the walls and in rows throughout the entire room à la a library or home center.

■ Line some or all of the walls in any of these spaces with pegboard or another specialized wall system and hang as many of your tools as possible. This will allow you to see what you have and keep your home repair supplies in better condition.

A SPACE FOR EVERYTHING A basement can be used for more than storage: The TV room *top*, and on page 88, occupies only one corner of a basement, leaving space for an exercise area. The garage *above* incorporates a specialty wall system that holds sports equipment, gardening supplies, and outdoor furnishings. See page 80 for more ideas from this garage.

■ Baby food jars are great for storing tiny screws and nails. If you secure the jar tops to the underside of a handy shelf, you will be able to open the jars using only one hand.

■ Industrial shelving is much less expensive than the better-looking varieties made for clothes closets and kitchens. These units can usually hold a heavy load and are ideal for tools and automotive and gardening supplies.

■ Because basements can be damp, avoid storing your stuff in cardboard cartons. Heavy-duty plastic or rubber bins are better choices below ground. For even better protection, avoid storing anything directly on the floor in a basement.

■ If your large storage boxes are opaque, inventory and number each box and keep a copy of the inventory on your computer or in a file paper. It may also be helpful to draw a diagram of the stored boxes; this will make it easier to locate a particular box when you need its contents.

■ For safety's sake, store items at least 2 feet away from your furnace.

■ Keep all solvents and chemicals where children and pets can't reach them.

■ If you ride your bike frequently, a wall rack in your garage will keep it handy. If you only take it out for a spin a few times each year, buy or build a pulley system that will keep it at ceiling height.

■ Large wire bins are great for storing sports equipment; industrial wire trash cans also work.

STAY ORGANIZED

■ Avoid the lure of warehouse club supersizes. Unless you are feeding an army, the food in those extralarge packages will turn stale before you use it up. The savings on toilet tissue by the gross are not large enough to justify the room they take up unless you have unlimited storage space.

■ Tackle one fix-it project at a time, moving on only when you have completed the project you started. If you see that you are in over your head, swallow your pride and call in a professional to bail you out.

■ As you seal boxes for storage, mark that day's date on them. Date a box again whenever you use any of its contents. Periodically go through your storage boxes and identify those that have not been opened in more than two years. Dispose of them immediately, without even bothering to open them.

■ When your children are grown and living elsewhere, start charging them rent to store their old stuff at your house. You'll be amazed at how much less attached they are to their high school class notes when they're paying by the square foot to keep them.

■ Resist buying secondhand or tag sale items that require repairs unless you are an expert and plan to work on the project that day. Otherwise you may never find the time to fix the item, and it will gather dust and take up space in your garage, basement, or attic. The same goes for furnishings that require reupholstering or refinishing and other projects that require your time, money, and effort.

■ Instead of buying every tool you might need for every project, borrow what you need from a friend or rent tools from your local home improvement center as needed.

PACK LIKE A PRO

If you are storing breakable items, such as glasses and dishware, wrap them properly before packing them in containers: Wrap them in newspaper, bubble plastic, or another protective covering. Make small stacks within a container and use only sturdy containers to avoid crushing.

■ If your garage is small (or your car is big), you may not have room for storage between the car doors and the garage walls. Instead hang shelves or even cabinets for rarely used items near the top of the garage walls.

■ To build easy storage for long items, screw shelf brackets to the studs. Fishing poles and golf clubs can be laid right on the brackets (no shelves needed). Similarly slender items such as rakes and shovels can hug the wall when hung on inexpensive hooks.

■ When building or installing storage in your garage, leave a clear path in front of the electric eye that helps operate the garage door opener.

■ Look high for storage opportunities in your garage: There may be space above the garage door where ready-made shelving units can fit. Use this out-of-the-way storage for seasonal or infrequently used items. Install the shelves carefully so they don't impede the functioning of the door.

@ FOR MORE IDEAS ON ORGANIZING YOUR GARAGE OR WORKSHOP, VISIT WWW.HGTV.COM/ORGANIZED.

HGTV MISSION: ORGANIZATION **65**

REAL HOMES, REAL CHALLENGES—AND REAL SOLUTIONS

I n the previous two sections you learned a tried-and-true three-step process for decluttering your home and you read expert advice on sorting and storing your possessions. Along the way you've learned why it's important to keep your home organized and you've gleaned strategies for keeping things neat and tidy after the sorting and storing is complete. Now you have an opportunity to see how professional organizers on *Mission: Organization* have helped homeowners turn hopeless-looking, chaotic spaces into orderly rooms that function well—and that the homeowners and their friends and families enjoy spending time in.

On the following pages you'll find tips from the professionals to help you clean out your problem space—and you'll undoubtedly learn lessons from the homeowners too. You'll see how they've overcome their personal barriers to make their homes more beautiful, organized, and livable. The 12 spaces featured in this section are arranged by organizational strategies, from creating "zones" in multipurpose spaces to managing space wisely in a small room. This will help you identify the rooms that most closely resemble your own. So sit back, relax, and read on— you may find the motivation you need to jump-start your own mission!

IN THE ZONE

IS YOUR LIVING ROOM MOONLIGHTING AS A HOME OFFICE? IS YOUR BASEMENT A FAMILY ROOM AS WELL AS EXERCISE CENTRAL? IF MULTIPLE ACTIVITIES HAVE OVERWHELMED YOUR AVAILABLE SPACE, YOU'VE COME TO THE RIGHT PLACE.

When your space needs to serve more than one function, dividing it into different zones is a smart solution. These zones may become reality with the help of permanent walls, movable partitions, and folding screens, or they may be signaled by a change in wall color or flooring. Sometimes merely grouping like items together can create effective zones.

The four spaces in this section prove that a multipurpose area can be an organized, tidy area. The apartment on page 70 utilizes wall color and ceiling-hung curtains to create specific areas for work, leisure activities, and dining. The garage that's featured on page 80 incorporates a ready-made wall system that helps keep lawn and gardening supplies, sports equipment, and more off the floor; it also provides space to park a car or two! The basement on page 88 offers areas for relaxing, playing, and exercising. And the home office on page 96 has plenty of space for three adults to work yet also makes room for relaxation.

MODERN-MINDED LIVING Leather furnishings and sleek accessories create a hip sitting area, replacing the ratty college-era items that were scattered about the apartment. Function is still key: The coffee table, for example, can be raised to cocktail table height for entertaining.

MAKING A SMALL APARTMENT WORK

THIS MESSY APARTMENT WAS SUFFERING FROM AN IDENTITY CRISIS, UNSURE WHETHER IT WAS A HOME OR AN OFFICE. WITH HELP FROM A PROFESSIONAL ORGANIZER, IT FOUND ITS TRUE CALLING—AS BOTH.

Whether you work from home full time or occasionally surf the Web and pay bills, there's little doubt that technology has thrown homes into a work/life conundrum. This home took the office concept to the extreme: The entire apartment was a warehouse of computers, software, tools, and papers that littered floors, covered tables, and created chaos on shelves. In short it was all work and no play.

It would have been easy for the occupant, a computer consultant, to pin the mess on the computer revolution. Yet the problem ran deeper than hard drives and motherboards. "By nature, I'm just not a neat person," he admits.

To the rescue came professional organizer Mela Catanzaro, a firm believer in the buddy system. "Whenever you're uncluttering a home, you never want to go in by yourself," she says. "Have somebody to support you."

SITUATION

- Papers, computers, and other work-related items litter floors and tables; no thought is given to organizing or even to putting things in neat piles.

- Space is limited; the public areas are essentially a foyer and a living room.

- Furnishings and accessories are holdovers from college days and no longer function for a young businessman.

SOLUTIONS

- Sort, sort, sort. Designate areas for like items and bring in storage containers that keep sorted items from slipping back into chaos.

- Create a separate living area and an office, using curtains to section the main space. Turn the foyer into a dining area that makes a good first impression.

- Purchase new furnishings, including a sofa to accommodate guests and sleek tables for office work space. Add items that serve multiple functions and expand storage options.

BEFORE

SORT THINGS OUT

Ignoring the bigger mess (starting small is always the best approach to getting organized), Mela set her sights on an old dining table turned dumping ground. Boxes labeled for mail, CDs, computer hardware and tools, and trash—four categories the occupant said would likely be found in the clutter—set the sorting in motion. Rather than starting at the top of the pile, Mela advised digging to the bottom to tackle the more difficult, long-forgotten things first. When the occupant began throwing things into a pile outside the four boxes, Mela asked him to put the items in whatever labeled box most closely described them, thereby preventing a potential new heap from forming.

The sorting continued in fits and spurts—a closet here, a built-in shelf there. A fragile album filled with old family photos, found on a cluttered shelf, was deemed valuable enough to get its own sorting box; Mela didn't argue this one. Even with team organization the owner has the final say; the helper's role is to assist when the owner is struggling to differentiate

MEALTIME With the apartment neatly organized, this new dining table *below left* escapes the fate of its predecessor, which was littered with so much paper and computer-related gear that it wasn't fit for feasting. Butted up to the wall, the table doesn't impede traffic to and from the doorway. Mirrors make the area feel spacious and allow quick grooming upon entering or leaving the home. **SEEING CLEARLY** A closet that formerly stowed a hodgepodge of items, including canned food, is now tools-only territory. Labeled plastic bins *below right* in a variety of sizes keep the owner's computer-repair and other work-related essentials at the ready. Flimsy shelves were replaced with deeper, sturdier ones to accommodate as many bins and as much weight as possible.

NIFTY NICHE In its former life this built-in niche was a catchall for printer parts and old family photos. With the clutter cleared and a few accessories added, it's a striking display area that also serves as a depository for small items as the owner enters and leaves the apartment. A decorative bowl on the bottom shelf holds mail. The two rattan baskets on the shelf above hold keys and other grab-and-go items.

BEFORE THE MAKEOVER The dining table *below left* was formerly covered in unopened mail and paperwork—and the clutter even extended under the table and to the floor. The nearby living room *below right* suffered from a similar fate and was furnished with unfortunate pieces that were neither comfortable nor appropriate for get-togethers with friends.

sentimental things that deserve special attention from items that can be safely tossed.

Other discoveries demanded almost instant attention. Canned goods stored with tools in a closet were moved to the kitchen. An uncashed check found under a chair and dollar bills strewn on the floor in one corner brought Mela to address money matters. "We want to have you become responsible in handling and managing your money," she tells the owner. "You're a high-end computer consultant." The solutions are easy: Mesh storage containers about the size of a bill offer an easy way to corral loose cash, and a filing cabinet with a folder designated for checks ensures income won't waste away under chairs.

Because the goal was to make the apartment feel like a home, the decluttering extended to the furnishings. Worn chairs and accessories that had served the occupant well during college were designated as trash.

PANEL DISCUSSION The red curtain panels that frame the arched doorway do more than add color and style: They act as a dividing line—a subtle reminder to keep living room items in one area and dining-related items in another. The patterned band on the bottom of the panels coordinates with the fabric on adjacent curtains that separate the living room from the office area.

WORKADAY WONDER A large desk would have taken up too much space in the office area; this slim, sleek table fits perfectly. A matching table in the opposite corner provides space for the owner to build and repair computers. The shelving unit and a $159 filing cabinet, which is set on casters for ease of use, compensate for the lack of desk drawer space.

DIVIDING LINE A ceiling-mounted curtain slides closed to separate the living room *above left* from the office area *above right*, creating two rooms out of one. The curtain makes it possible to hide work in progress if unexpected visitors stop by; it also helps keep business out of mind at the end of the workday.

VISUAL CUES

Faced with the challenge of melding working with living—and not letting the two collide—Mela had to rethink the floor plan. At 19x16 feet, the main room wasn't small, at least not by apartment standards; however, it was the only true public room in the place.

Mela's ingenious strategy carved three functioning rooms from what was essentially one space. The walk-through foyer area was made into a stylish dining room that makes a good first impression; a new table replaced one that was too cluttered to be used for dining. The front of the main room was turned into a space for relaxing and watching television, while the far end of the room became the office.

Knowing the occupant was prone to letting things get jumbled, Mela employed design tricks to help remind him that items need to stay in their respective areas. She used a curtain on a ceiling-mounted rail to divide the living room from the office. When closed the curtain creates a private living room and keeps reminders of work out of sight—an important feature for anyone hoping to strike a healthy work/life balance. Curtain panels also flank the doorway leading from the living room into the dining area to mark the separate functions of the two spaces. "Some people think curtains are just for windows, but we put them here so he knows that everything on this side of the curtain stays in the living room, and everything on the other side of the curtain stays in the dining room," Mela says. "And it actually happens to be pretty."

The freshly painted walls offer more visual cues to aid in organization. The back wall in the main room is painted blue, a departure from the green used elsewhere, to designate that this is the office.

MIND GAMES

It helps to be in the right frame of mind when decluttering, says professional organizer Mela Catanzaro. Before you hunker down, treat yourself to a good meal and then put on some comfy clothes. If the phone rings, let your machine answer it. If you're disciplined, allow yourself 15-minute breaks every few hours and minicelebrations to mark completed goals. When your organizational willpower starts to wane, crank up the tunes. "Just so you don't feel like it's going on forever, put on some of your favorite music, and then bang it out like nobody's business," Mela says.

TAKE A STAND Three-shelf metal stands flank the sofa to provide display and storage space. The remnants of an old photo album that was formerly left on a shelf in the entry find shelter in one of the jute canvas boxes. About $22 each, the boxes are a stylish way to keep clutter at bay.

SMALL CHANGES, BIG REWARDS

Even small changes make a big difference. To economize space, Mela transferred the owner's computer CDs from their original jewel cases into ultraslim cases, doubling the number of CDs that can fit in his bookcase. The pantry-style closet is now outfitted with stronger, deeper shelves to accommodate more items. Furnishings were chosen for their ability to pull double duty. For example a new coffee table converts into a cocktail table. In the dining area the now clutter-free niche is a tidy landing spot for mail, keys, and small items that may be needed when leaving the apartment.

"The difference is like night and day," Mela says. "Before, when you walked in there, the place was complete and utter chaos. I thought, 'Oh, what am I getting myself into?' But now it's magnificent. It's like a VIP club." The occupant pays his new space a bigger compliment: "It's a home, not a warehouse," he says.

FILLING STATION

If your ideas for staying organized are running on empty, consider this strategy: Let storage containers guide you. To tame the occupant's habit of stashing dollar bills on the floor in a corner near a spare-change jar, professional organizer Mela Catanzaro invested in a $1.99 mesh container that was the same size as a bill. She placed it in the office area to provide a tidy landing spot for loose cash. When the container is filled, it's a sign to cash in at the bank. Apply the same strategy to other items: When the bowl, basket, or bin is full, it's time to take action.

HOME OFFICE HELP

A home office must be an organized environment. Ideally it encourages creativity, aids productivity, and helps efficiently accomplish the task at hand. Divide the space into zones to ensure that it is hardworking, not merely good-looking.

■ **Zone One.** This is the immediate work area and contains essential materials arranged for easy access. A calendar, telephone, pens, notepads, and computer are common essentials that are best kept no more than 30 inches away from the desk chair. Frequently used phone or reference books can be kept on a bookshelf or in a cabinet that's connected to or near the primary workstation. The work surface itself must allow enough room to work on projects or pay bills.

■ **Zone Two.** Items that get only occasional use can be placed several steps away from the primary work area. If space allows put these items on shelves and in filing cabinets around the perimeter of the room. In a kitchen consider designating one cabinet for office items. If your office is an armoire-style computer station in a living room or bedroom, maximize storage with ottomans that have lift-up tops, end tables that have drawers, or a trunk that rests at the foot of the bed or serves as a coffee table.

■ **Zone Three.** The final zone is for nonessential items. Because most home offices are strapped for storage, find other areas of the home to stow infrequently used items, such as supplies you've purchased in bulk or old tax records. Designate an inexpensive plastic or metal shelf in the basement or the upper two shelves of a linen closet for extra office-related items.

GARDEN ZONE Positioned near a door for easy access to the yard, a handy lawn and garden zone organizes often-used items on hooks and shelves. A bin on the bottom shelf holds seed that formerly spilled from a bag onto the floor—and that birds had discovered and freely feasted on. Inexpensive plastic bins are an easy way to keep fertilizers, grass seed, and bird feed free from moisture and away from pets and children.

REGAINING A GARAGE

THIS CLUTTERED GARAGE WAS DRIVING ITS OWNERS CRAZY. WITH CREATIVE STORAGE SOLUTIONS THAT TAKE ADVANTAGE OF EVERY INCH OF WALL SPACE, THE THREE-STALL STRUCTURE IS NOW AS HARDWORKING AS IT IS GOOD-LOOKING. AND THERE'S EVEN ROOM FOR CARS!

G arages, like many basements, get no respect. They can be a dumping ground for objects evicted from other rooms of the home, a labyrinth of unruly garden hoses interspersed with sporting goods, or merely a place to shelter a car. To professional organizer Vicki Norris, a garage can be so much more: It has the potential to be a tidy extension of the home with vast storage possibilities and even space for a vehicle or two.

BEFORE

When Vicki encountered this garage, it was bursting at the seams. With the husband being a garage sale junkie and the wife an avid gardener with lots of equipment for yard work, the clutter had become overwhelming. "There's so much stuff," one homeowner says. "We don't really know what to do with it and we don't always agree on what to do with everything, so we just don't deal with it at all."

SITUATION

▨ No logical organization: Gardening supplies intermingle with sports equipment and furniture.

▨ The garage is filled with never-used items, including bedroom furniture and gardening tools found at garage sales and secondhand stores.

▨ The floor is covered by miscellaneous objects. The garage is useless for auto storage.

SOLUTIONS

▨ Create zones to keep the garage in order: Designate separate spaces for gardening supplies, sports equipment, and patio furnishings.

▨ Evaluate the condition of stored items, and either throw away or donate unwanted possessions.

▨ Build out the stone walls with a specialty wall product that accommodates racks, hooks, and bins; this will open up floor space for cars.

EDIT TO MAKE ROOM FOR WHAT YOU LOVE

Vicki's first order of business with the wary couple was to debunk a common myth many people have about organizers. "A lot of people think a professional organizer is going to come in and say, 'You must throw this away,'" Vicki says. To the contrary Vicki considers herself an "advocate" whose role is to help homeowners make room for the things that are important to them, not to rid them of all their possessions.

Still some whittling is involved; editing is an essential part of every successful organizational project. In this case large items—including a bedroom suite, a dated upholstered chair, and exercise equipment—were obviously crowding the three-stall garage. Vicki offered a challenge: The owners needed to find spaces inside the home for the items or be willing to sacrifice garage space in order to keep them. If they couldn't agree to either, she recommended donating the items to a charity. To show she was serious, she arranged for a truck to come to the home the next day to transport any unwanted but usable items.

BEFORE THE MAKEOVER Garage sale finds, such as an old bicycle in need of repair *above left*, consumed valuable floor space in this garage until a wall-hung storage solution was introduced *opposite*. Lawn and garden supplies *above right* were formerly strewn throughout the garage. Now they are organized in a special lawn and garden zone shown on page 80.

SURFACE MATTERS Plastic is the material of choice in a moisture-prone area such as a garage. Plastic shelves add grab-and-go convenience in this recreation/sports zone. Elevating items above the floor prevents them from getting wet and makes floor cleanup a breeze. However, not every garage is shelf- and bracket-ready. The stone walls in this garage made it difficult to attach hardware, so they were covered with thermoplastic panels ($10 a square foot), part of a garage organization system that includes cabinets and hooks. The floor was updated with a stain-resistant $5-a-square-foot covering that's pounded into place.

HAVE A SEAT In many locales leaving patio furniture outdoors year-round is an invitation for rust, mildew, and sun damage. Brought into the garage and elevated, these iron chairs and matching table find a nifty hibernation spot that will extend their life span. Hung on padded metal hooks (which protect against scratches), the chairs become artful assets and won't have to be moved when it's time to clean the floor. Stored on its feet, the table would occupy too much floor space. Instead it finds a space-conscious home on the wall.

SORTING

SORTING

BEFORE THE MAKEOVER
Sorting like items gives you an accurate view of what you own and how much space the items will occupy in a newly organized room. Making signs for common categories *above and left* will ensure that like items stay together.

SORT, STACK, AND TOSS

With the larger items having found new homes inside the house or being donated, it was time to tackle the smaller, seemingly more manageable things. Paper signs taped to the wall designated the sorting categories the couple planned to use (such as yard and garden, memorabilia, and sports equipment). These signs helped the couple start down the road to organization.

The homeowners learned a hard lesson: Cardboard boxes and moisture-prone spaces don't mix. A box of photos stored in the garage had become wet, turning the photos into a mildewy mess. "I really recommend you keep paper goods indoors," Vicki says. "And we also don't want to keep them in cardboard. We want to put delicate papers in something weather resistant."

MAINTENANCE PLAN: KEYS TO SUCCESS

Getting organized is only half the battle; the other half is staying organized. Follow these tips to ensure that you stay the course:

■ **Consider your surroundings.** Every room has different needs. A garage, for example, needs storage containers and shelving that can withstand water, insects, and temperature fluctuations. Think plastic, not cardboard, so your efforts—and items—aren't ruined by the elements.

■ **Stay in the zone.** Once you've designated an area for specific items, keep it that way. Storing a suitcase on a shelf in the garden zone may seem harmless, but eventually such choices can snowball into an unorganized mess.

■ **Be flexible.** Choose cabinetry and shelves that can accommodate your changing needs. If an existing shelving unit isn't adjustable, shop for racks or stacking bins that will enhance the function of the unit.

■ **Make things easy on yourself.** Keep frequently used items in an easy-to-access spot. Take the guesswork out of locating stored items by using clear plastic containers. Professional organizer Vicki Norris used such containers to organize holiday decorations stored in the third stall of this garage.

■ **Do a reality check.** View a change in seasons as an opportunity to assess your space. If you enjoy bicycling, for example, keep your bikes within reach during the spring and summer months, when you will use them the most; in fall and winter position the bikes higher on a wall and move other equipment, such as skis, to a lower, easy-to-reach place.

UPWARD MOBILITY The old builder's maxim that it's more efficient to build up than to build on holds true with this garage, which puts vertical space to good use. A weather-resistant locking cabinet acts as a safe for charcoal and other items that could be harmful to children or pets. With its glass top removed, even the patio table finds a secure, high-up home; the area between the table legs accommodates folding chairs. Space beneath the workbench comes in handy for tall items.

CABINET MEETING Storage containers inside this cabinet *above left* organize items into minizones. When shopping for cabinets, look for those with adjustable shelves; the flexibility is worth the extra cost. This cabinet is an ultraorganizer: An adjustable door bin slips between two shelves when the door is closed. **DURING THE MAKEOVER** A team of professionals *above right* installs the space-saving wall unit and durable flooring.

DESIGN TRICKS MAXIMIZE STORAGE

To maximize the vertical storage space in this garage, Vicki called in a team of experts to build out the stone walls with a material that would easily accommodate the hooks and hardware needed for hanging. Stain-resistant flooring was installed to protect the floor from spills and to allow easy cleaning.

Designated zones cleverly corral specific items. The recreation/sports zone, for example, features a shelf that keeps balls and skates readily accessible—an improvement over having to dig through a huge plastic bin. In another area out-of-season patio furniture hangs high on a wall, freeing up floor space. Elsewhere a tall cabinet keeps charcoal and other unsightly items hidden behind closed doors. Everything hugs the walls, leaving plenty of space for vehicles.

LESSONS LEARNED

Vicki's message definitely helped the owners clean up their act. For starters, they learned to part with items that were doing nothing besides gathering dust or mildew, including the bedroom furniture they inherited from a relative. "Other people might have been able to use that, so it makes more sense to give it to charity than to have it sitting in our garage," the wife says.

Doing his part to maintain the tidy new look of their garage, the husband vowed to stop braking for garage sales. "I know I would go by and pick up stuff and bring it to my garage," he says. "I don't want my garage to look like that ever again."

SLEEP TIGHT There's more to this table than meets the eye: The panel it's attached to swings down to become a bed. At $4,000 this convertible table/bed wasn't cheap. However, it gives the family valuable, much-needed guest space. Positioned in a back area of the basement as part of the "game zone," the unit usually serves as a game table.

BUILDING A BETTER BASEMENT

THIS MESSY FINISHED BASEMENT HAD BECOME AN EMBARRASSMENT FOR ITS OWNERS—AND EVEN THEIR KIDS. NOW IT'S A FRESH, FUN HUB OF THE HOME WITH ACTIVITY AREAS THAT WORK FOR THE ENTIRE FAMILY.

F inished basements offer some real advantages; this basement, however, had turned into a curse. Action figures, castles, dolls, and science projects belonging to the couple's three children had taken over, rendering the entire lower level almost useless. "I would literally spend two hours straightening up and I still had other things to do, so I just got to the point where I said, 'You know what? Forget it!'" one owner says.

Enter Crystal Sabalaske, a professional organizer who is known for her inventive use of space. Where the owners saw clutter running amok, Crystal saw stylish activity areas that both the parents and kids could enjoy and smart storage to encourage everyone to keep the place in order.

BEFORE

SITUATION

■ Toys are strewn everywhere, making it difficult to navigate the room. Large pieces of exercise equipment also take up floor space. A shelving unit has become a clutter catchall.

■ The room has no clear function, and the objects in it have no designated home within the space.

■ Dark paneled walls make the space uninviting.

SOLUTIONS

■ Sort and group like items. Remove the shelving unit; use existing built-ins, new storage containers, and a closet for storage. Group exercise equipment together to form a minifitness center.

■ Create "activity zones" to give each area a distinct purpose.

■ Brighten the dark paneling and built-ins with paint to make the basement more appealing to the entire family.

BEFORE THE MAKEOVER Toys and more toys occupied most surfaces in the basement *above left* prior to the organizational makeover. **GAME TIME** A wicker trunk stores toys and doubles as a coffee table in the "game zone" *above right*. The top of the trunk offers a surface for playing board games; otherwise it's kept clear for easy access to its contents.

FIRST THINGS FIRST

Before you splurge on the latest storage system or even a dozen plastic crates, stop! "You can't know what your system is until you know how much you need to store," says professional organizer Crystal Sabalaske. Whatever condition your room is in, sorting comes before shopping. Remove the contents of drawers, cabinets, and closets and then organize them into piles of like items. Once you have a clear idea of the sizes and types of things you own, you'll be able to look for storage units that are suited to specific items. See pages 25 to 30 for more information on choosing storage containers.

HOMEWORK TIME

To ease the family into the organizational process, Crystal gave them an assignment: Walk around the basement and find things to put in a "donate" pile. Pleasantly surprised by the results when she returned—though the basement was still brimming with stuff—Crystal moved on to the next step: sorting. "We need to clearly define what's going on in this room," she says, explaining the purpose of sorting. "When you're organizing, work on one area at a time." Otherwise, she adds, "it can be pretty overwhelming."

Signs taped to the wall designated areas to place things belonging to the parents, the kids, and the family in general. Another sign—"trash"—designated the spot for a crucial organizing category. All damaged, broken, and unusable items were to report there for pickup.

Letting go can be tough, yet Crystal managed to persuade the parents to part with some sentimental favorites, including a painted little girl's chair. "Give it to somebody else," Crystal tells them. "Your kids had a great time with it, but you need to make room for them to have a good time with their new stuff."

HAVE A SEAT A $73 table paired with built-in benches makes the spacious passageway between the television and game areas a functional place to do homework or crafts projects. Formerly magnets for clutter, the benches are now inviting and comfy thanks to fresh white paint and new red cushions.

SITTING PRETTY Topped off with shelves and a television, an existing built-in cabinet becomes a focal-point entertainment center in the "movie zone." A fresh coat of white paint makes it "pop" against the blue wall. A washable slipcover updates the existing sofa.

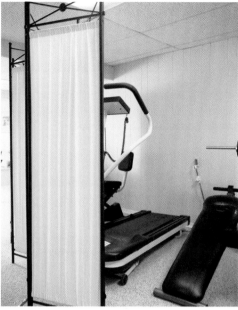

BEFORE

BEFORE THE MAKEOVER Before professional organizer Crystal Sabalaske came to the rescue, the "home gym" *above left* looked more like a playroom with a few exercise machines in its midst. CLEVER COVER-UP Lightweight folding screens keep exercise equipment out of sight *above right* and can be easily moved when the owners want to work out. The machines are strategically placed so exercisers can see the television in the "movie zone" during workouts.

MAKING ARRANGEMENTS

As the clutter was eliminated and the sorting completed, Crystal began to get a clearer vision of how to arrange things. She also had time to assess what wasn't working. A large shelving unit that served as a room divider seemed like a nifty storage place; however, it was actually allowing the family to haphazardly stuff it with whatever fit. "The shelves were catching clutter, which is what we don't want," Crystal says. In addition the unit was aesthetically unappealing and made the space feel too closed in, so it was eliminated.

Crystal's plan melded function with style. The function came in the form of "activity zones," designated areas for watching television and movies, exercising, playing games, and working on crafts projects or homework. In the "movie zone" an existing built-in desk unit with lower cabinets offered space for movie storage. Small toys found a home in a newly cleared closet and in wheeled storage bins that the kids can easily roll out into the game area. Large toys were left out in the open and tucked under a countertop, giving an awkward, underused nook new purpose.

As for style, the basement came alive with the power of paint. The dark paneling and built-ins were coated with a light, bright, cheerful personality, so the newly organized basement is even more appealing and thus more likely to be well-maintained.

PICTURES

PICTURES

BEHIND CLOSED DOORS Organizing goes beyond surface level. Labels adhered to the shelves inside this cabinet offer a handy reminder of what goes where, encouraging everyone to return favorite movies to the correct spot. (If you want kids to pick up after themselves, choose storage places they can easily reach.) Similarly the labeled boxes on top of the cabinet take the guesswork out of what's inside. The green storage bin tucks nicely into place in what was once the kneehole of the desk.

FUNCTION JUNCTION

Pretty storage boxes and baskets need to offer more than good looks. Remember the old designer's maxim: Form follows function.

■ As much as possible, store items in the area where they'll be used. Otherwise, after you retrieve an item, you may never get around to putting it back.

MAINTENANCE PLAN

The owners were surprised that Crystal was able to find a place for everything, as promised; they were equally surprised at the payoff from one basic concept: labeling. Labels identifying the contents of storage containers and shelves make it easy to locate items and encourage the kids to put them back later. "If they can't find something, I'll say, 'Well, did you put it back where it belongs? If not, I don't want to hear about it,'" one owner says. Adds Crystal, "[Maintenance] doesn't happen overnight. Once you have a system, it needs to become a habit."

■ Strive to maximize the function of a space. For example, to encourage use of a treadmill, position it near a window or television. Place unsorted photos in boxes on a coffee table and sort them while watching TV.

■ Make items easy to retrieve. Wheeled storage containers are handy for items that need to be moved elsewhere for use. A suitcase with wheels is a nice option for storing everything from dolls to scrapbooking supplies. Consider adding casters to wooden crates or furnishings to make them portable; old drawers, for example, can be turned into rolling underbed storage containers.

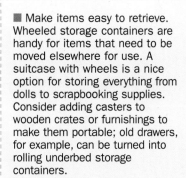

BEFORE

BEFORE THE MAKEOVER Though the videocassettes were placed in a centralized location, they were far from organized.

■ If you must store items on high shelves, keep a step stool or small ladder nearby. (Foldable step stools can be stored behind doors.) Store items in clear plastic containers or in labeled bins to make it easy to find what you need.

@ VISIT WWW.HGTV.COM/LABELS FOR EXCLUSIVE LABELS YOU CAN PERSONALIZE.

HGTV MISSION: ORGANIZATION 95

WARM-UP TIME Earthy golds, reds, and greens and rich wood tones warm up this formerly stark room. It's now a comfy sitting area that showcases the home decor products one of the owners sells.

HOME OFFICE TRIUMPH

IT'S OFTEN DIFFICULT TO CARVE OUT OFFICE SPACE IN A HOME. WHEN YOU NEED TO CREATE A HARDWORKING SPACE FOR TWO PEOPLE INVOLVED IN DIFFERENT BUSINESSES, THE CHALLENGE BECOMES EVEN GREATER. WITH A SMART NEW LAYOUT AND EFFICIENT FURNISHINGS, THIS DUAL OFFICE GOES FROM WORKADAY TO "WOW."

BEFORE

You only get one chance to make a good first impression. If a client had stopped by this home office, the impression would have been one of chaos and confusion. It was a space where a husband and wife involved in two separate businesses tried to work amidst toddlers' toys, a finicky feline who had claimed a desk chair as a napping spot, and a plethora of papers scattered on the floor. "As my business has grown, my office and filing systems have not grown accordingly," the husband says.

Indeed, business was booming: The husband's contracting business brought in a bounty of blueprints, and boxes of products arrived daily for the wife's home decor venture. "It's not working anymore," the husband says. "The more we grow, the more we need a better system."

This space offered unique challenges, but professional organizer Vicki Norris was ready to get down to work. "You're both going to have your own space," she tells the couple.

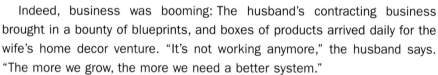

SITUATION

- The room has no boundaries between work and play. The space is a blur of toys, computers, papers, and boxes.

- The existing office furniture and the layout fail to meet the needs of three workers (the husband has one employee).

- The room lacks style.

SOLUTIONS

- Designate the room as an office. Relocate toys to another area of the house. Store some of the boxes in the garage.

- Improve the function of the room by creating individual work spaces for the couple and another space in the husband's area for his employee. Purchase new desks and storage units.

- Turn the stark space into an environment conducive to work, using earthy colors, fresh fabrics, and rich wood furnishings.

DISCOVER AND CONQUER

Perhaps the most agonizing part of any decluttering mission is figuring out where to start. "Good organizing is about a discovery process, so we're not going to know everything at once, and that's OK," Vicki says. "We're going to do what we know first."

What the couple knew was this: The toys, the boxes of products for the wife's business, and the furnishings that didn't add function had to go. With those items relocated to other rooms of the house, it was time to tackle the unknowns cluttering desk drawers, tabletops, shelves, and the floor. "We need to unravel this whole nightmare," Vicki says.

The sorting started with an obvious category—office supplies—and grew as new discoveries warranted more categories. Each sorting box was clearly labeled so the sorters could avoid confusion about designated categories. "Once we get about 20 boxes, we'll be happy we have the labels," Vicki says.

CHARITABLE ACT

Good intentions of donating items to a charity are sometimes sidetracked, and the items end up in a box or bag in the basement. To avoid this scenario, categorize items as you sort them and then toss the bags or boxes into your car. Professional organizer Vicki Norris explains, "You're going to be much more motivated to actually take them to the charity of your choice because they're taking up car space."

SHARED SPACE The husband's desk spans a back wall of the room and provides work space for his bookkeeper, who formerly shared a desk with the wife. A shelf that spans the desk holds a fax machine, a printer, and project files. The portion of the desk that juts out from the wall forms a cozy nook on the other side, where clients can pull up a chair.

BREAK ROOM This stylish spot functions as a reception area. It's the first thing visitors see when they enter the room and it's a bridge between the two office areas. The sofa is actually a daybed that occupied the office before the makeover.

MIX STYLE WITH FUNCTION

To give the room the comforts of home and a businesslike atmosphere, Vicki blended style with function. Stark white walls were splashed with three earthy colors to visually warm up the space and give the different areas their own identities. The husband's office now sports golden walls, while the wife's space at the opposite end of the room is green. A cozy sitting/reception area with walls painted gold and rusty red bridges the space between the offices.

Desks were chosen for both form and function. The wood tones add a rich look; the function comes from matching filing cabinets that tuck underneath and a shelf that expands the storage space on the desk top.

Though some of the old furnishings reappeared, they're barely recognizable. A daybed was called into action as a sofa in the sitting area. In the husband's office a cedar chest that was used as a printer stand stores rolled-up blueprints that formerly piled on the floor. A freshly painted black table that anchors the community workstation is accustomed to serving a crowd; it used to be a shared desk.

TURN THE TABLE Professional organizer Vicki Norris took advantage of the architectural features of this room to create semiprivate work areas, such as this community workstation *above left*. The table, formerly a messy shared desk for two workers, offers space for collating and compiling packets. New paint freshens the table; lamps flanking a container of office supplies add a homey touch. BEFORE THE MAKEOVER Large spaces sometimes encourage disorganization; when a space has room for everything, everything moves in. This spacious office *top and above right* was in disarray until Vicki stepped in to help bring order to the chaos.

WORKING SMARTER

Overworked and out of time? A few simple tweaks in your workday can lessen the stress:

■ When deciding whether to file something or pitch it, consider the words of professional organizer Vicki Norris: "Eighty percent of the things we file, we never look at again."

■ Be realistic when making a "to do" list. A list of 15 tasks invites frustration and a sense of failure, whereas a list of 5 can be a motivator. If you struggle to limit your "to do" list, create a "must do" category and focus on those tasks first. Eventually you'll have a sense of how much you can reasonably complete in a day. Having an organized office will help you cross things off sooner.

■ Skip the fancy color-coded filing system or any system that demands too much attention or time. Find a system that works for you. It may be as basic as categorizing papers into manila folders and handwriting labels.

GET DOWN TO BUSINESS

From every vantage point, the room is now a model of efficiency. Desktop organizers keep pending projects and everyday office essentials within reach. Other work-related projects are filed in cabinets close to the desk chairs, while personal items are housed in the filing cabinets a bit farther away.

"It's set up just perfectly," one owner says. "Everything is right where we need it. It's very organized. I think it will streamline everything and make work go much faster."

 **BEFORE THE MAKEOVER** Before professional organizer Vicki Norris came to the rescue, this home office was filled with toys and boxes, and the furniture layout wasn't conducive to a productive work session *top left* and *above left and right*. **DURING THE MAKEOVER** Vicki and the owners of this office begin the task of sorting *top right*.

PERSONAL SPACE The husband's drafting table found a home between the window and the built-in shelves across from his desk. The shelves keep a smattering of reference books handy and still have room to display a few personal items.

GOING UP These desktop organizers embrace the concept of vertical storage. The $139 "project center" on the left offers quick access to pending projects and frequently used supplies. The $199 "action center" on the right functions like a "to do" list. Anything coming into the office that needs attention goes onto the most appropriate shelf (the shelves slide out), so nothing gets lost in the shuffle.

ELECTRONIC ORGANIZATION

Keeping a home office looking good and functioning well requires regular management of computer files and equipment. Consider these tips for taming the tide of technology and all its trappings:

■ Set up electronic folders by project or by client; save all the information that pertains to the task or client within that electronic folder. Get in the habit of saving documents under logical file names, such as "letter/jane doe" and "letter/john smith," so they'll be easy to find if you need to refer to them.

■ Back up files at least once a week by copying data to a CD, disk, or other storage medium. The time it takes to back up data is minimal compared to the headache you'll have if your computer crashes. Keep backup CDs or disks in their own special storage space or label them clearly so you're not tempted to grab one when you're in a pinch for copying everyday data.

■ Organize disks into book-style binders or containers specially designed for them. Use a tiered desk organizer or a wicker storage basket as a temporary holding spot for CDs and disks until you have time at the end of the week to put them in the appropriate binder or container.

■ Schedule 30 minutes at least once a week to tend to computer equipment. Purge old files, check for documents that have been saved in the wrong areas, and back up files. Replenish paper in the printer and fax machine. Dust the monitor and keyboard.

■ Resist the urge to keep the boxes your computer, printer, and fax machine were packaged in. If you just feel you must keep them, at least disassemble them so they fold flat and take up less storage space.

■ If you have an old computer that's not in use, check with a school or charity to see if the hardware can be donated. (With identity theft on the rise, it's crucial to get rid of documents stored on the computer hard drive before you donate.) If the computer isn't in working condition, check with your city to see what regulations it has for trashing computers. Or check the phone book for computer recyclers.

 **GOOD FORM A** home office calls for storage that goes beyond basic metal shelves. With its weathered good looks, this cabinet fits the bill. The cabinet stores food items and accessories that are part of the wife's business, yet its unbusinesslike appearance is a welcome addition to the office environment.

A FAMILY AFFAIR

ORGANIZING YOUR OWN POSSESSIONS IS CHALLENGING ENOUGH. DEVELOPING STORAGE SOLUTIONS THAT WORK FOR EVERYONE IN YOUR HOUSEHOLD CAN BE DOWNRIGHT DAUNTING. HOWEVER, IT CAN BE DONE, AND YOU'RE ABOUT TO LEARN HOW!

Finding a place for everything you and your family use and enjoy—from games and toys to hobby-related items—is easier said than done. That's where this section can help: It will teach you how to carve out space where you can store and easily retrieve your stuff at a moment's notice.

On the following pages you'll find three families with spaces in desperate need of an organizational overhaul; you'll also find dozens of ideas to turn your own problem spaces into rooms that look great and function well for everyone. The garage on page 108 uses a system of hooks and bins to keep sports equipment, gardening supplies, and more off the floor yet within easy reach for kids and adults. The passageway on page 118 accommodates both a laundry area and a play place; leading from an attached garage into the house, it also functions as an attractive entryway. The basement bedroom on page 126 offers two boys plenty of space for sleep, play, and homework—and even the closet is neat and tidy.

CLEAN SCENE This garage shows what smart organization—and the proper storage units—can accomplish. Most of the items that were once strewn about the garage remain. However, they now have a home off the floor, on gridded hanging storage racks, cabinets, and shelves. The center pole separating the two stalls got a facelift: It is now bright yellow, and the lower portion is wrapped with a padded mat for safety and to prevent vehicles from getting dings.

TAMING AN OVERACTIVE GARAGE

LOADED WITH BALLS, BATS, BIKES, SKATES, AND MORE, THIS GARAGE SEEMED LIKE A SPORTING GOODS STORE—AND A MESSY ONE AT THAT. ORGANIZER GENEVIEVE SNYDER HITS A HOME RUN WITH A MAKEOVER THAT KEEPS THE SPORTS GEAR AND LOSES THE CLUTTER.

BEFORE

Looks can be deceiving. With the garage doors down, this home was the picture of perfection. With the doors open, however, the mess inside canceled out the curb appeal. "I always try to keep my garage doors shut because I'm so embarrassed the neighbors are going to drive by and be like, 'Oh my gosh, this family must be slobs,'" one owner says.

Slobs they are not, at least not in the couch potato, sit-around-and-do-nothing sense. The parents love sports and outdoor activities, and their three young children are following in their footsteps. However, their active lifestyle took a toll on the garage: Piles of sneakers littered the doorway to the house, footballs and basketballs were scattered about, bicycles took up valuable floor space, and the only cars that could park inside the garage were pint-size plastic ones.

"The mess is creating tension," the other owner says. "It's tough to maneuver, coming home from work with no lights. I close the door and forget about it."

SITUATION

■ Sporting goods and kids' toys have taken over the garage. Cars cannot be parked inside.

■ The large space isn't being used efficiently. A wooden shelf unit is too big and difficult to access.

■ The owners keep procrastinating on cleaning up the garage.

SOLUTIONS

■ Install hanging racks and a storage system that can hold all the sports equipment, thereby freeing up floor space for cars.

■ Create vertical storage on the walls and a 3-foot-deep space at ceiling level. Remove the bulky shelf.

■ Put owners to work with a systematic plan for sorting and organizing. Add storage units and some fun painted designs to inspire them to treat the garage with respect.

YARD WORK The painted message on the wall says it all: This area is devoted to lawn care. The same grid-style wall rack used for the sports area works here too. The ladder hung horizontally above the unit can be reached by using the step stool that resides near the left end of the rack.

CREATE CATEGORIES

At 23 feet wide and 19 feet deep, this garage had plenty of space. However, it was packed full, and unfortunately for Genevieve, the family used nearly everything that was stored there. This meant she had to find a handy home for a plethora of items.

Because it was difficult to navigate in the overcrowded space, Genevieve and the owners concentrated on sorting and clearing one small area to free up space for a more thorough sorting. The ultimate goal was to create three storage areas—one for lawn and garden items, one for toys and sports gear, and one for home maintenance and household items—with room left over for two vehicles.

LAYERED LOOK Layering like items or those with similar shapes, such as these shovels, is an easy way to gain storage space. Use hooks that are beefy enough to accommodate the combined weight of your items.

Genevieve's systematic approach—taking things in small steps and completing small areas before moving on—made the huge task seem less daunting. Items were first sorted into piles designated as "keep," "relocate," "charity/yard sale," and "trash." Then the latter three piles were moved out of the garage (still separated by category to avoid the need for re-sorting) to free up more working space. The "keep" pile was then divided into the three main categories—lawn care, sports gear, and home maintenance—some of which were then subdivided into seasonal categories.

"It's probably going to get uglier before it gets better—it's always darkest before the dawn," Genevieve says as the owners make their way to the other side of the garage. "Don't get discouraged. You're almost there, and it's going to be so worth it."

START SMALL

In the workplace experts usually advise tackling the toughest jobs on your "to do" list early on. It's the opposite with organizing. Start with the small stuff and ease yourself into the more challenging tasks. By the time you get to the tough stuff, you will have freed up space to deal with it, and you'll likely be motivated by the results of your earlier effort.

MOD AND MODULAR This grid unit keeps favorite sports gear tidy and can be easily changed to accommodate different gear as interests change. The activity baskets can be repositioned on the unit, as can the clever in-line skate racks, which cost about $60 each.

A PLACE FOR EVERYTHING

Because the majority of the items needed to remain in the garage, Genevieve had to concentrate on using all the space efficiently. She delivered with a smart plan that maximized storage by using walls and even the ceiling. "I am in utter shock," one owner says of Genevieve's savvy solutions.

Bicycles—a big floor hog in any garage—found new homes on a wall-mounted grid system. Adjustable wire baskets and racks now hold baseball bats, balls, and other sporting goods. Another modular unit organizes the lawn care area, keeping rakes and shovels neatly in place. "With this system it's very easy to change and adapt to new things," Genevieve says.

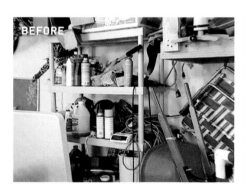  

BEFORE THE MAKEOVER An exposed shelf unit *above left* **was a landing spot for everything and anything, including insect repellent and windshield washer fluid. RISING HIGH Wire shelves fill in the gap between two cupboards so there's no wasted storage space** *above right*. **High spaces are great for items that get infrequent use or for items such as fertilizers and insecticides that could harm pets or children.**

SLIM FIT To squeeze the maximum into any space, consider the most efficient way to store your possessions. Hung vertically, this skateboard takes up a fraction of the space it would use if it were stored on a horizontal shelf. Baseball gloves also hang in a row from hooks for grab-and-go convenience.

UP, UP, AND AWAY Bicycles can take up a lot of floor space, especially when every member of the family has one. This space-saving grid system gets the bikes off the floor yet offers easy access when the family is ready for a ride.

The most creative use of space appeared overhead: Two ceiling-mounted storage units were hung above the railings for the automatic garage doors. "It's wasted space," Genevieve says of this often underutilized area. Though she had only a 3-foot-high space to work with, she was able to gain enough storage space to accommodate seasonal and seldom-used items.

Equally inspired are the decorative touches Genevieve added to give the utilitarian space a homier feel. Bright red and yellow paints punch up the door that leads into the house, while signs and motifs painted in bold colors on the walls identify the three main storage areas.

With everything in a designated place, the garage is now a source of pride; the doors can stay open without causing embarrassment. Even the children seem inspired. "When they're done playing, they're cleaning up," one owner says. "They're putting the balls where they should be, and I'm helping them put the bikes back on the hooks."

LETTING GO

What to toss and what to keep—it sometimes takes a neutral party to help you decide. One case in point in this garage was a hefty wooden shelf the owners had built. It was a nice attempt to keep things organized, but professional organizer Genevieve Snyder pointed out that it was too large for the space and also had become a cluttered catchall. "It took us over a week to build," one owner pleads when Genevieve put it on the chopping block. In the end they trusted her instincts and wound up with much more functional—and flexible—shelving units. It also took trust on the owners' part (and prodding from Genevieve) to give up smaller things that were only gathering dust. "If you haven't used it in a year, then it's probably a good thing to say goodbye to, and chances are you'll never miss it," Genevieve tells them. "You might want to kick me once or twice, but for the most part, you'll be happy that you can get your cars in here."

LOOKING UP Wasted space is nonexistent in this garage. Genevieve put 3 feet of unused headroom to work with ceiling-mounted storage racks *above left*. Each rack holds seasonal items, such as lawn chairs and beach gear, that can be retrieved with a ladder when needed. PAINT AWAY Gallons of leftover paint fit perfectly in this six-cubby storage unit *above right*. Painting supplies are stowed in the lower cubbies. Grouping like items together is a cardinal rule in getting—and staying—organized.

TV TIME By building out a wall in the laundry area, the family gained this cozy nook for watching TV. A built-in entertainment and storage unit, with a desk area that doubles as a child's work space, tucks between the walls. Framed photos add a homey touch; placed on higher shelves they're safely out of reach of curious kids. Beanbag chairs are an inexpensive, portable, and kid-friendly alternative to traditional chairs.

TIME TO WORK, TIME TO PLAY

THINGS WERE SUCH A MESS IN THIS MULTIPURPOSE ROOM THAT IT WAS DIFFICULT TO TELL WHERE THE PLAYROOM ENDED AND THE LAUNDRY ROOM BEGAN. WITH A BIT OF CONSTRUCTION AND PARING DOWN, THE BOUNDARIES OF EACH ARE CLEAR, AND THE OWNERS ARE NO LONGER AIRING THEIR DIRTY LAUNDRY.

At one time or another, almost everyone has had a room that is best shut off from the world—perhaps a guest bedroom that has become a dumping ground for old furniture, or a home office littered with papers. In this home the trouble spot was a spacious playroom/laundry area. Shutting the door and forgetting about it wasn't an option, though, because the space was actually a passageway to the attached garage. Every time the owners walked through, they were reminded of projects that had never been crossed off their "to do" list. "It's always a mess," one owner says. "We have the worst time trying to keep it under control."

BEFORE

Many people may rationalize that—like peanut butter and jelly—kids and clutter go together. Professional organizer Sean Johnson disagrees. "Organizing is like problem solving," Sean says. "It's putting together a puzzle. If you treat it like a game, kids get excited."

SITUATION

■ The two functions of this space—playroom and laundry room—collide. Toys and dirty clothes are everywhere.

■ The space lacks storage units, and the number of toys is excessive.

■ The large open space lacks character and purpose.

SOLUTIONS

■ Enclose the laundry area to differentiate the two distinct functions of this space.

■ Sort, edit, and group toys by category. Introduce baskets for storage.

■ Build out a wall to enclose the laundry area, thereby creating a nook for a TV space. Carve a mudroom out of one corner. Warm up the space by painting the walls yellow.

BASKET BRIGADE Two straw baskets with fabric liners and handles make lightweight toy chests that can be safely stacked to conserve space. They're also stylish enough to grow with the family. Down the road they can store a burgeoning CD collection or blankets and pillows for sleepovers.

WASH DAY Double doors close off the newly organized laundry area *above left*, **a spiffy version of its former self** *above right*. **The carpeting was cut out and replaced with more-appropriate tile flooring, and a new washer and dryer moved in to make the cleaning chore seem less cumbersome and more efficient. New cupboards store detergents and items that never had a real home, such as tablecloths that once sat on the floor for weeks, waiting their turn to be washed. The goal was to create a laundry room that would encourage prompt cleaning, folding, and storage of clothing and other washables.**

LEARN TO WHITTLE

Sean focused on turning the parents into organizational role models, figuring the example would trickle down to their kids. Her strategy started with sorting, and she steered the parents to tackle one small area at a time. Toys were sorted into categories: throwaways, keepsakes, and giveaways. To avoid resorting and rehandling of items, she instructed the owners to group as they went. Doctor-theme toys, for example, were placed in one sorting bag and dolls in another.

Sean was equally straightforward about paring down. "I always encourage less is more," she says. That philosophy even extended to the clothes hampers in the laundry area. Sean suggested getting rid of them because they were an invitation for the laundry to pile up; she advised the owners to put dirty clothes directly into the washing machine. The children's books also underwent her scrutiny. Rather than filling every inch of a bookcase, she limited the number of books that were brought back in. Her strategy was this: Don't overwhelm a child by offering too much, and don't add extra cleanup time putting back books a child will inevitably pull out. "You'll be surprised," she says. "The more you pare down and keep the things the children really play with, the happier you'll be, and the happier they'll be."

TACKLING TOYLAND

Let's face it: Most kids have too many toys—way too many toys. Donating toys to a charity, a needy family, or a friend down the block is a kind act and a great way to clear clutter. If you're not ready to part with certain playthings, pare down by removing some toys from the play area and keeping them out of sight in the basement or a closet. Every now and then reintroduce some of the toys. "It's like Christmas all over again for a child," professional organizer Sean Johnson says.

ADULT SUPERVISION Some items are better stored out of children's reach. Professional organizer Sean Johnson purposefully stored the children's movies high enough on the shelves to require adult assistance. The jute canvas boxes, which cost $20 each, keep the videos from getting misplaced or damaged and help maintain order. The ends of the boxes pull open for easy retrieval of the contents.

(THOMAS)

(GRACE)

SET BOUNDARIES

With the clutter cleared, it was time to create zones to define the various functions of the multitasking space. The 21½x14-foot room was essentially one big box, so Sean devised a plan for changing the shape, both structurally and visually.

The first task was to create a hardworking hidden laundry area so the washer and dryer (and piles of clothes) would no longer be a focal point. Building out a wall and adding double doors to enclose the machines required the skills of a contractor; however, the final result was well worth the expense. The rectangular room was turned into an L-shape space, with a nook ideal for TV watching. More important, the family gained a designated laundry room, essential for their long-term organizational maintenance plan.

Other zones were carved out in more subtle ways. In a corner near the door leading to the garage, Sean had the carpet cut away and replaced with tile flooring to create a mudroom area. The owners had recognized the need for a landing spot for coats and shoes and had previously attempted to create one. Sean, though, took the mudroom concept to a stylishly new level, with strategically placed coatracks, a storage bench, and wicker baskets for easy organization. Adjacent to the mudroom, an informal library area features a bookcase the children can easily access and space for pulling over a beanbag chair from the TV area.

Golden yellow walls warm up the formerly stark room; the color appeals to both kids and adults. "It's a child's playroom, but it's also a family room," Sean says. "As the years progress, you want the room to convey that."

LANDING ZONE Rather than fight the fact that family members tend to drop things wherever they happen to enter the home, embrace it. Sean Johnson carved this hardworking and stylish mudroom out of a corner between the kitchen and the garage door. Durable and easy-to-clean tile flooring replaces worn carpet in this high-traffic area. The new floor surface visually separates the mudroom from the rest of the space and breaks up the boxiness of the room. A coatrack hung at toddler height encourages the kids to hang up jackets, a mirror offers adults a chance to check their appearance before rushing out, and a bench provides a convenient spot for changing footwear.

NAME GAME Fabric-lined baskets feature each child's name so everyone knows where things belong; this quick trick also encourages the kids to take responsibility for picking up after themselves. Shoes are piled into a basket and slid under the bench—a tidier approach than letting them haphazardly pile up in a traffic path. At about $170 the wooden bench was a bargain, offering a place to sit as well as drawers to hold hats and gloves.

GRACE

THOMP

DECORATING DOS

Give some thought to the decor of your room and your organizational efforts will really shine. Design and organization are more closely related than you may think, so factor in these tips:

■ Paint it pretty. Paint is the easiest and least expensive way to change the mood of a room. A soft earthy green, for example, sets a calming tone, even in a busy room. Avoid jarring colors you may quickly tire of and ones that are gender- or age-specific. Otherwise you'll have to repaint prematurely, which means moving your furnishings into temporary quarters—and then reorganizing the room all over again.

■ Present a united front. Use leftovers from your decorating projects to embellish storage boxes and bins. This will give your room a coordinated look. Wallpaper, fabric scraps, and unused paint can dress up storage boxes or wicker baskets. Easy-to-sew fabric liners add style to baskets; if you don't sew, look for baskets with ready-made liners that coordinate with your room.

■ Furnish wisely. Get in the habit of looking for little extras when shopping for new furnishings. A bench or a coffee table with drawers is a wise investment, as are ottomans that offer storage space within.

KEEP IT CLEAN

The sunny yellow walls are a bright spot in the reconfigured and reorganized room. The new washer and dryer and storage cabinets in the laundry area are also a happy addition. "I actually enjoy doing the laundry a little bit now," the husband admits.

Both owners say that Sean's prodding them to pare down—something they initially resisted—was also key to the success of their mission. The excessive number of toys, which they now realize overwhelmed their children, has been reduced, and everything that remains has a home, so the kids know right where to find their favorites.

"Because we had so much work into this project, we feel we have some sense of duty to keep it neat," one owner says. "We enjoy the room so much more when it looks better." But that's not to say pickup duty is the sole responsibility of the adults in this home or any other. "I think that most parents make the mistake of cleaning up after their children, just because they think their kids can't do it," Sean says. "But it's a learning experience. It doesn't have to be a perfect room, but at the end of the day, [children should] put the toys back in the containers and put them back on the shelves or cabinets."

DOUBLING UP Chairs by day and beds by night—furnishings that pull double duty are a boon in any room. The cabinet between the chairs serves as a nightstand when the chair seats are folded out into mattresses. A towering rattan cabinet that stands nearby helps divide the sleeping/relaxing area from the work area and provides extra storage.

SLAM-DUNK BEDROOM

TWO ACTIVE BOYS IN ONE SMALL BEDROOM RARELY ADDS UP TO A TIDY ENVIRONMENT. HOWEVER, THE TWO YOUNG SPORTS FANS WHO OCCUPIED THIS BASEMENT BEDROOM JOINED IN A TEAM EFFORT TO ORGANIZE THE SPACE. BRIGHT PAINTS, SMART FURNISHINGS, AND MORE MADE THE ROOM A WINNER.

When two siblings share a bedroom, it can mean double the mess and double the stress. When the siblings are at different stages in their lives and have different interests, the problems are compounded. In this room the 13-year-old, a budding engineer and artist, had claimed the lone desk. The 8-year-old had dibs on the television.

BEFORE

Unfortunately they did have one trait in common: "They're both messy," the mother says, and the boys agree. The fact that the room was in the basement—out of sight and out of mind—didn't help either. "I haven't taken the time to go down and help them with organization," the mother says.

For professional organizer Janet Taylor, the challenge was to create one look that reflected both boys' personalities, while giving each of them individual space. To help transform the long, narrow room, she enlisted interior designer Deana Murphy, whose goal was to add fun and function.

SITUATION

■ The shared bedroom is crowded and doesn't meet the individual needs of the two boys.

■ The disorganized closet makes it difficult for each boy to find his clothes.

■ The basement room is dark and has no style—almost inviting the boys to let the space slide into chaos.

SOLUTIONS

■ Replace old furniture with more-functional, space-saving pieces, including two chairs that convert into beds.

■ Designate specific areas of the closet for each boy; establish a system for keeping it organized.

■ Paint the walls with bright colors and add sports-related accessories to inspire the boys to take pride in their room and keep it clean.

CORNER OFFICE A tiered desk makes creative use of a corner in the work area. The desk belongs to the teenager, who needs more work space than his younger brother. New overhead lighting and a lamp bring much-needed light into the space.

FIND MUTUAL INTERESTS

Staunch believers in letting children have a say in their rooms, Janet and Deana sought input from their young clients. New furnishings and new paint for the walls—orange and blue emerged as mutual favorites—were on the boys' wish lists.

To make way for the new, though, much of the old had to go. An initial sweep of the room got the toys and clothes off the floor and the furnishings and cleared the room of everything the family didn't want to keep. A company that hauls away household junk (charging by volume) took the hassle out of disposing of the large furnishings the parents decided to part with. "Having us here helps them realize that they could actually have their space back," one of the movers notes.

Deana's spirited design called for bold paint colors to visually divide the bedroom into two areas: a working space with two desks and a sleeping/relaxing area. Painted stripes and a diagonal design on the walls designate the latter space, while solid-color walls define the work space. Sports-related accessories throughout play up the boys' mutual interest.

Though bunk beds are the conventional choice for doubled-up bedrooms, Deana chose an alternative that saves more space: two chairs that convert into twin-size beds. When they're folded into the chair position, they leave plenty of floor space for the boys and their friends to hang out and watch TV. The youngest boy was skeptical about this unconventional bed. "Once he really gets to understanding what's going on, I think he'll love it too," the mother says—an acknowledgment that involving kids in a room makeover doesn't mean handing over the reins.

BOLD MOVES When the boys said orange and blue were their favorite colors, interior designer Deana Murphy listened. She added cinnamon and white for more variety and depth; the white also helps brighten the dark room. A diagonal design on one wall of the sleeping/relaxing area offers visual relief from the stripes. The accessories, including $15 pillows in football, basketball, and soccer ball shapes, make it clear that the boys are serious sports fans.

FUN AND GAMES

Getting kids to tidy up their space is easier if you choose storage containers that inspire fun. Putting dirty clothes in a hamper becomes a game if the hamper is in the form of an over-the-door basketball hoop; wicker baskets for toys also inspire hoop dreams. A colorful mesh hanging bag on a wall-mounted peg rack provides a handy spot for storing stuffed animals or dolls. Think of unconventional ways to spark a child's desire to clean up. However, if you select large freestanding furniture—such as a metal locker to inspire sports-minded tykes to hang up their clothes—secure the unit to the wall for safety.

SLAM DUNK This closet scores big on kid-friendly design. An over-the-door hamper acts as a basketball hoop, making a game of picking up dirty clothes. A pants trolley can be rolled out for easy retrieval of slacks or jeans. Modular cabinets add a locker-room feel to the closet. Hanging clothes are grouped by color, and two different hanger colors designate which items belong to which boy.

CREATE A KID-FRIENDLY CLOSET

For Janet the challenge was to restore order and establish a system that would encourage long-term tidiness. Her approach was to get everything out in plain view and then sort it into categories. "I'm hoping 60 percent is trash, 30 percent is give-away, and we keep 10," the optimistic mother says of the piles of toys, shoes, and clothing heaped on the floor.

Whittling the wardrobe of two growing boys was the most daunting task. The boys tried on clothes so their mother could check for fit and decide if some articles of clothing could be handed down to another son or pitched. "Throw it away, throw it away, throw it away," she urged when one boy uncovered a pair of old sneakers.

The underutilized and inefficient closet warranted extra attention. Janet knew it had to accommodate the boys' belongings and the mother's busy schedule. "I want to maximize the closet space so she can organize the clothes that they have, get rid of the things they don't need, but also set up a system that will help them help her keep everything organized," Janet says.

Making the space user-friendly was essential to the plan; the current system wasn't working. Janet decided to designate a portion of the closet for each boy. That way shirts, socks, and shoes would not intermingle and cause confusion.

Two modular units, one for each boy, were brought in to store everyday items, with space for shoes on the bottom shelves, drawers for shirts and undergarments, and open cubbies for frequently worn items. Seldom-worn items were relocated to the shelf above the hanging rods. One of the modular cabinets was positioned on a long wall below the clothes rod to create a barrier between the boys' hanging clothes. Two colors of hangers—blue for one child and white for the other—lend more distinction.

"Now I can see the clothing, so now I know what colors they have; I know how many shirts, how many pants—whereas before, everything was just all bunched up and I had no idea," the mother says.

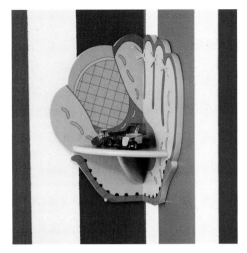

GOOD CATCH Like the desk shown on page 128, this glove-shape shelf *top* makes clever use of a corner. It also offers display space for a few small toys. BEFORE THE MAKEOVER Before the addition of modular storage and a color-coded hanger system, the closet *above* was a jumbled mess.

CLOTHES CALLS

When you're organizing a closet bring in a full-length mirror and try on seldom-worn garments that you're having a hard time parting with. When you see the item on you, rather than on the hanger, you may instantly decide it's not worth keeping—or happily discover you have a new favorite item. Kids usually dislike trying on clothes; however, because they outgrow items, it's a must. Schedule a "fashion show" before the school year starts. Donate unwanted items or store them for a younger sibling.

ALL'S WELL THAT ENDS WELL

The closet is a big hit with the mother; the boys rave about their brightly colored sports-theme bedroom. The convertible chairs that one boy doubted turn out to be one of his favorite things because they're perfect for watching TV with friends. Removing a bulky dresser opened up room for two desks, so each boy has space for his own projects. An armoire and other storage units organize toys and other belongings. "The boys are happy, and the room is awesome," the mother says.

STYLISH STORAGE Embellished with painted balls and stripes, this armoire *top* is a sports-minded storage unit. To get a custom look without a custom price, unite mismatched furnishings by painting them all the same color. Then add details that fit the color scheme and theme of a room, using stencils or decorative techniques such as stripes. DURING THE MAKEOVER Professional organizer Janet Taylor *above, left* reviews her plans for the bedroom with the two young occupants and their mom.

DONATING DOS AND DON'TS

Almost every decluttering mission includes a trip or two to a charity to drop off unwanted items. Make the most of your donations with these tips (see page 20 for additional ideas):

■ **Do** make some calls to find out where your items arc most needed; you'll feel better and have more incentive to purge. Check beyond widely known charities. A local church may have a family in need of furniture, a women's organization may be seeking office attire for women entering the workforce, or a nursing home may be in need of blankets.

■ **Do** schedule an appointment if a charity calls to say it will be in your neighborhood—even if you're not sure what you might donate. Pickup services are an ideal no-cost way to get rid of large items, such as an old sofa or dresser. Even if you donate only a few boxes of clothing, you'll have cleared some clutter.

■ **Do** ask for a receipt, which is needed for tax-deduction purposes. Put all charitable receipts in a folder so they're at your fingertips at tax time. Get a receipt even if you're not sure if you'll deduct the donation. (See page 21 for a handy chart that will help you keep track of your tax-deductible donations.)

■ **Don't** donate items that are in poor condition. Otherwise the charity will have to waste its resources in discarding the items.

■ **Don't** drop off items that the charity might not accept. Find out in advance if the organization takes old computers, treadmills, and other unconventional items. Also ask about clothing restrictions; some groups take only in-season clothing.

■ **Don't** drop off items when the charity is closed, unless a sheltered after-hours drop-off spot is clearly designated. Call in advance to find out if you need to go to a particular entrance; ask what times donations are accepted.

CLOSED FOR THE DAY This slim cabinet-style desk unit takes up mere inches of floor space in the 8½x16-foot room. The work surface folds up, and the chair can be moved elsewhere so the boys have an open court for shooting hoops on the closet door. Painted stripes and sports motifs customize the $190 desk.

SMALL SPACE, BIG IMPACT

SMALL ROOMS PRESENT SPECIAL CHALLENGES FOR ANYONE ON AN ORGANIZING MISSION, ESPECIALLY WHEN THE SPACE NEEDS TO HOST MORE THAN ONE ACTIVITY. HERE YOU'LL FIND SOLUTIONS TO HELP YOU MAXIMIZE ORDER AND FUNCTION IN ROOMS WITH LIMITED SPACE.

Large rooms have advantages: They offer more flexibility for furniture arrangement, and they can host more activities and more people than smaller rooms can. However, with more space comes the potential for more clutter. That's where small spaces may have an advantage: Limited floor space forces clutter to find another home, so (theoretically) occupants of small spaces are motivated to edit their belongings or to devise clever storage strategies for their stuff.

On the following pages you will find three rooms that are small in square footage yet big on style and function. The bedroom on page 136 incorporates space-saving furnishings and savvy storage solutions to provide its 25-year-old occupant with a multipurpose home/hangout. In the apartment featured on page 146, one little room serves as a bedroom, living room, and office. Color combined with an ingenious layout makes the room live large. The bathroom on page 154 may be big in comparison to some baths; still it offers lessons that are sure to help you make the most of your bath, regardless of its size.

ON THE MOVE Conventional design rules call for placing a bed in the center of a room, clear of windows, to make it a focal point. Some rules are meant to be broken: Placing this bed against a wall and window opened up floor space and created a sleeping space with a view. The 25-year-old occupant now has plenty of room for friends to hang out. This smart use of space allowed professional organizer Betty Kim to bring in filing-cabinet cubes that double as a bench.

A BEDROOM GROWS UP

THIS BEDROOM SPILLED OVER WITH CHILDHOOD KEEPSAKES THAT NO LONGER FUNCTIONED FOR ITS YOUNG ADULT OCCUPANT. THOUGH LETTING GO OF THE PAST WAS HARD, A MOTHER-AND-DAUGHTER TEAM FINALLY SETTLED ON A PLAN TO TAKE THE ROOM FROM GIRLY-GIRLY TO GROWN-UP. SMART STORAGE SOLUTIONS AND SAVVY USE OF SPACE MAKE IT A ROOM WITH STAYING POWER.

BEFORE

A child's bedroom is a special sanctuary, a place for daydreaming and make-believing. So what do you do when the child grows up and is still living in a room with dolls and a rocking horse?

The challenge for professional organizer Betty Kim was twofold. First was the task of turning a little-girl room into a living and sleeping space suitable for a 25-year-old. The second challenge was to referee a mother-daughter tug-of-war between the past and present. The mother wanted to hold on to sentimental items from her daughter's childhood. The daughter, living at home to save money, wanted to make room for her computer, television, and other grown-up gadgets. "A lot of things I want to throw out are the things she doesn't want to throw out," the daughter says. "And a lot of things I don't want to throw out are the things she says, 'Oh, you can get rid of this, get rid of that.'"

Consider the impasse a rite of passage. All parents and children experience similar growing pains, be it a transition from nursery to toddler room or when a child heads off to college and the room is turned into a guest room.

SITUATION	SOLUTIONS
■ Clothes and shoes are spilling out of the closet, covering furniture and the floor and making it difficult to find what's needed to dress for the day.	■ Get rid of seldom-worn items, move coats and jackets to a downstairs closet, and build a custom storage unit in the bedroom closet to keep things organized.
■ Trinkets from childhood and college no longer suit the occupant, who is now a young working woman.	■ Create hanging display space for a few thoughtfully chosen childhood and college mementos.
■ The room needs to function as both a bedroom and living quarters.	■ Remove some of the little-girl furnishings and reposition the bed to gain floor space. Create space for a home office/entertainment area.

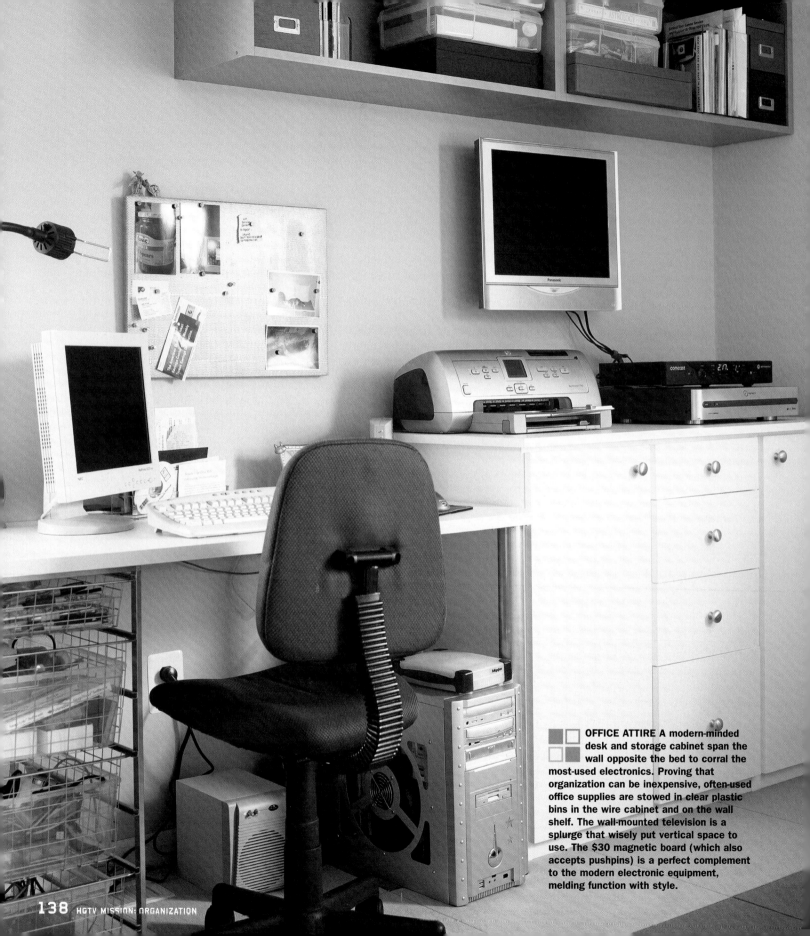

OFFICE ATTIRE A modern-minded desk and storage cabinet span the wall opposite the bed to corral the most-used electronics. Proving that organization can be inexpensive, often-used office supplies are stowed in clear plastic bins in the wire cabinet and on the wall shelf. The wall-mounted television is a splurge that wisely put vertical space to use. The $30 magnetic board (which also accepts pushpins) is a perfect complement to the modern electronic equipment, melding function with style.

THINK BIG AND START SMALL

Though the goal was to create a grown-up space, the process involved lots of baby steps. "Start with the small stuff," Betty urges. In this case a jumble of music and computer CDs was one of the easy and uncontroversial starting points.

Armed with her favorite organizational tool—plastic trash bags—Betty had her team designate two additional bags, one for charity and one for "maybes," items whose fate would be negotiated at a later date.

When her team seemed unable to even attempt to tackle one side of the bedroom, Betty broke that down into baby steps too: The mother and daughter looked at the area as a whole, with an intimidating cluttered closet; Betty had them focus solely on a wicker chair that had become a dumping ground for clothing. Sorting came first—

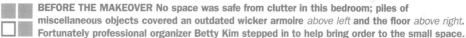
BEFORE THE MAKEOVER No space was safe from clutter in this bedroom; piles of miscellaneous objects covered an outdated wicker armoire *above left* and the floor *above right*. Fortunately professional organizer Betty Kim stepped in to help bring order to the small space.

CD AND DVD STORAGE

Keeping CDs and DVDs in their original cases or boxes is usually a drain on space and an invitation for disarray. Professional organizer Betty Kim recommends storing the discs in zippered or notebook-style CD folders. "It's much more compact," she says. Use one for music CDs, one for movies, and one for computer software. The folders offer grab-and-go convenience. If you're heading out for a road trip, for example, one folder holds your collection of tunes. If you must keep the original cases, find a storage box designed for them or place them in a plastic bin with a lid so you have a place to return the CDs when you're done using them.

TUNED IN Stereo equipment and cases full of CDs occupy a sleek rectangular storage unit. Grouping like items in one area is an easy way to keep things organized. When choosing new furnishings for a room, look for those that offer flexibility. This unit could be used as a bench, set vertically and outfitted with shelves to create a slim bookcase, or hung horizontally on a wall and used as a shelf to save floor space.

OUT WITH THE OLD

It's all too easy to let clutter creep back into a newly organized space. To prevent that from happening, follow this rule: Whenever you bring something new into a room, get rid of something old. A bedroom is an ideal place to put this rule into practice, because it's especially easy to apply the rule to clothing and shoes.

coats and jackets, for example, were moved to a downstairs closet. This eased the mother and daughter into the weeding and editing process. When they finished uncovering the chair, Betty got a better look at the piece and moved it out of the room for good.

The larger tasks soon followed. If clutter has reached epic proportions, as it had in the daughter's closet, the only way to proceed is by settling in and prodding bit by bit. Sometimes pleasant surprises emerge: The daughter discovered $40 in an old birthday card. However, sometimes, even with baby steps, backsliding occurs: The mother couldn't resist rescuing a few items from the trash bag. Whenever this happened mother and daughter learned the art of compromise on what things should stay and what should go.

CLOSET CAPER Who needs doors when you have a storage system as stylish as the one in this closet? Leaving the doors off provides incentive to keep the closet tidy. Little touches, such as a framed photo on a shelf and the uniform white hangers that cost $1 each, help dress up the hardworking space. A small rod between the upper shelves can be telescoped to offer a handy hanging spot for assembling an outfit.

DESIGN TIME

Because the bedroom needed to serve multiple functions—essentially it's a miniature apartment for the daughter—Betty knew she had to put every inch of the room to good use. She carved out areas for sleeping, working, and hanging out, while also maximizing the closet space and finding space for some keepsakes.

A tidy, organized space is pleasant enough; if it's stylish to boot it may actually inspire the occupant to maintain order. To that end Betty splashed a calming green paint over the cutesy wallpaper and the ceiling and then painted a wide gray stripe across some walls to kick the design into high gear. Peel-and-stick carpet tiles in a mix of colors updated the flooring. Their modern and modular appearance set the stage for the sleek furnishings that followed. "If something happens, you can just pop out one and replace it," Betty says of the $10-per-tile carpeting.

With open floor space, a corner for sleeping, and a stylish office area, the room is now operating at maximum efficiency. The pièce de résistance, though, is the closet. Outfitted with a custom-built cabinet, adjustable shelves, and hanging rods, it fits the daughter's newly whittled wardrobe to a T. "All that remains has a home," Betty says. "It's a beautiful, clean, streamlined closet."

HAPPILY EVER AFTER

Despite the growing pains—or rather, the throwing-away pains—both mother and daughter are ecstatic about the end result. The daughter has gained a restful retreat she can enjoy after a long day at work. "Now I have a room where I can walk in, I can lie down, and I can relax," she says. "I don't have to worry about a huge mess."

Discarding is still difficult for the mother (she managed to hang on to a doll and stuffed giraffe, among other things). The daughter, however, is sold on the benefits. "The stuff that's gone, I probably didn't even know I had," she says.

Committed to keeping her new space organized and adult, the daughter has some friendly advice for her mom: "No matter how cute the stuffed animal might be, refrain from purchasing it for any holiday or birthday, because it's only going to collect dust," she says.

BEFORE THE MAKEOVER The closet *top* **was brimming with clothing, shoes, and shopping bags, while a nearby chair** *above* **was buried in clothing that wouldn't fit into the messy closet.**

OPEN-DOOR POLICY Echoing the wide gray stripe painted on some of the walls, this rectangular shelving unit is an artful addition to the room. It's also a clever way to extend storage space. Blue and green cardboard boxes keep some items hidden, while adding a spot of color. Clear plastic magazine holders keep reading material from cluttering the desk or floor; when a holder is full, it's a reminder to discard the contents to make room for the new.

CLOTHES ENCOUNTERS

If your vice is hanging on to old clothes, you're not alone. Even "fashionistas" can heed this advice from professional organizer Betty Kim: "We only wear a small percentage of what we have. The rest can be trashed, and you wouldn't miss it." When editing your wardrobe, keep in mind that people tend to wear 20 percent of their wardrobe 80 percent of the time. That means the bulk of any given wardrobe is gathering dust on hangers. Consider these tips to get a grip on your clothes closet:

■ **Size things up.** If it doesn't fit, get it out of the closet. Dress for the size you are now, not what you were a few years ago. If you end up losing weight and being able to fit into the smaller sizes, you'll probably want to treat yourself to new clothes anyway.

■ **Hang with the best.** After you've whittled the contents of your closet, treat the remaining pieces right. Padded hangers help keep sweaters from losing their shape, while clip-style hangers designed for trousers prevent unwanted creases. Hangers made of heavy-duty plastic or wood are low-cost luxuries that make a closet look better and thereby encourage you to keep it clean,

■ **Box it.** Put seldom-worn items in a box and put it aside. If you have no need to pull out an item in a year, your box is ready to give to charity. Limit the deadline to six months if you're really committed to paring down.

■ **Take inventory.** Make an honest assessment of what's in your closet. Remove any garments that need mending or cleaning and don't put them back until broken zippers are repaired, missing buttons are replaced, or stains are removed. Garments that have faded or lost their shape need to go too, as do shoes that are uncomfortable, beyond polishing, or merely unappealing.

HIGH-WIRE ACT Sheer curtains hung on a tension wire behind the sofa create a cozy cocoon for sleeping. When company calls, the panels can be closed to hide the makeshift bedroom.

FROM APARTMENT TO HOME

LACKING IN SIZE, THIS STUDIO APARTMENT NEEDED A LARGE DOSE OF SPIRIT AND A BETTER STORAGE PLAN. NOW DECLUTTERED, FRESH DECORATIVE TOUCHES MADE IT A PLACE THE OCCUPANT IS NOW PROUD TO CALL HOME.

BEFORE

This diminutive studio apartment crammed multiple functions—living, sleeping, eating, and working—into one lifeless space. "I have an apartment now that I eat and sleep in, and what I want is a home that I can live in," the young career-minded occupant says.

Unfortunately the apartment had few inspiring features on which to build homey happiness. It lacked a view, it had no architectural detailing to showcase, and it didn't get much natural light. In short the occupant had little to work with and a lot to make over. "I don't like to make mistakes, so I just don't do anything," she says.

Even self-professed "apartment therapist" Maxwell Ryan says that, from an interior design standpoint, "it's about as bad as you can get." From an organizational standpoint, though, there was hope. "This apartment doesn't need decorating so much as it needs undecorating," Maxwell says. "It needs to be uncluttered."

SITUATION

■ It's a studio apartment, with a tiny, crowded main room that has to function as a living room, bedroom, office, and place to dine.

■ The occupant has trouble parting with things. Piles of books and paper clutter the room.

■ The room lacks storage space and style. It gets minimal natural light, so it's dark and gloomy.

SOLUTIONS

■ Define the different areas. Hang curtain panels to section off the sleeping area. Remove furnishings that don't work well in the room and introduce new pieces that can serve multiple functions.

■ Sort and purge items. Move loose paper piles into stylish storage containers.

■ Add open shelving for storage. Brighten the room with paint and new light sources.

BOOK SMARTS An orange wall makes a bold statement yet stands back to let books take center stage. Placed in short stacks—rather than spanning the entire shelf in an upright row—the books let small color bursts show through. The book spines introduce more color and pattern in the room.

 **SPLIT DECISION** Apartment therapist Maxwell Ryan separated the large sofa into two sections that fit the scale of the space better. This chaise section faces the television to create a comfy viewing area. The slim lamp behind it offers light for reading and conversation.

BIG THINGS FIRST

The occupant traced her bad habit of piling things around the perimeter of her room to her genes. "My mom is a pack rat," she says. "My father tends to put things in piles. It's like an organized mess—little nice, neat piles of things. I tend to have that problem with all the things I keep."

In the name of a clutter-free home, she was ready to purge and to put her faith in Maxwell. "I find that getting rid of stuff is the complete solution to revitalizing your space," he says. "And that's where I have a tough time with clients, and that's why it's therapy."

Larger items were assessed first. Maxwell quickly saw that a table and chairs (pushed against a wall and piled high with stuff), a bookcase, and a CD holder were taking up precious floor space. He surmised that none were stylish enough to keep.

Smaller items, such as piles of papers and stacks of books, required individual sort-and-toss attention from the occupant. Once the process was complete, storage boxes and magazine holders—stylish enough to be left out in the open—were introduced to discourage new piles from forming. "Everything is going to look like you've taken care of it—it's organized and it's put away," Maxwell says.

PURPOSEFUL PURGING

If getting organized means you'll need to toss a good number of things, take an inventory of the main items in the room before you start. Decide on paper what to keep and what to throw out. To avoid spending too much time on the list, group smaller items into broad categories, such as "old college textbooks." The list will help you stay focused, and you'll be able to make quick decisions when the actual decluttering begins.

MAKE ROOM FOR COMFORT

Whether you're living in cramped quarters or have a grand space, apartment therapist Maxwell Ryan recommends the same approach for making the place homey:

■ Clean out your space. If you buy one thing, get rid of one thing.

■ Define your rooms to keep them orderly. For example use the bedroom for sleeping and relaxing, not for watching TV or surfing the Internet.

■ Use low lighting all around a room—and turn off the harsh overhead lights.

■ Use your home. Love it and enjoy it. It will get better the more you do.

QUICK CHANGES, BIG RESULTS

Maxwell's threefold design plan proved that decorating can do more than make a room look pretty. He organized, maximized, and stylized without big costs or a commitment to permanency. "The changes are quick and reversible," he says.

Curtain panels now create a soft wall between the living and sleeping areas, thwarting the possibility of paperwork creeping into the bedroom or clothes ending up in the living room. One wall of the living area was painted a warm, invigorating pumpkin color to brighten the lifeless space. The apartment door got a coat of the same orange paint to draw the eye down the long entry corridor; this trick makes the living area seem more spacious. Shelves hung on the orange wall provide to-the-ceiling storage in the newly designated office area, with the lowest shelves offering work

BEFORE

BEFORE

BEFORE THE MAKEOVER Every part of this small studio apartment *above left and right* **was covered in clutter before apartment therapist Maxwell Ryan came along to bring order to the chaos.**

ON THE HORIZON Painting the apartment door the same pumpkin color as the living room wall draws the eye down the 15-foot-long hallway, making the living room feel deeper and more spacious. Shelves that stretch to the ceiling maximize storage and display space.

space for a computer or paying bills. A large two-section sofa was separated and repositioned to create a cozy living room; a new coffee table that rises to dining table height joins the ensemble.

"We created a home that has depth and dimension and has many more possibilities than it had before," Maxwell says. And at long last the place really feels like home. "Before, I felt that it was a temporary space," the occupant says. "And now I have a whole home where I live, where I can spend time, where I feel comfortable. It just feels so much more whole to me."

PRESTO CHANGE-O A small space calls for versatile furnishings. By pressing the foot lever, diners can raise this coffee table to standard dining height. The glass and chrome table takes up less space visually than a wooden table would and also helps bounce light around the room.

LET THERE BE LIGHT Slim wall-mounted lamps cast a warm glow. The lamps are an artful alternative to end-table lighting; end tables are impractical in this small space.

SHOWER POWER This tub and shower combo saves on square footage yet squeezes in style with elegant tile, dressy fixtures, and a wooden surround. The deep tub offers a relaxing soak, while the shower is all about convenience. Towel bars go high and low, rather than side by side, to maximize space. Between the bars is a laundry chute that leads to a hamper in a hall closet. The chute replaces an unattractive hamper that took up floor space.

MASTERING A BATHROOM

SOMETIMES ORGANIZATION REQUIRES RE-CREATION. THIS BATH HAD SUFFICIENT FOOTAGE YET ITS OWNERS NEEDED IT TO FUNCTION BETTER. BY GUTTING THE ROOM AND STARTING FROM SCRATCH, THEY CREATED A STYLISH BATH THAT FULFILLS ALL ITS FUNCTIONS WHILE CURTAILING CLUTTER.

BEFORE

Thirty years ago this master bath impressed a house-hunting couple. They bought the house and settled in for the long haul. "I was wowed by the bathroom when we first moved here because it was so large," one owner says.

The bathroom was large indeed, with a 14x19-foot main area and closets in the entry space. It had a large soaking tub and a separate shower—amenities still favored in high-end baths. However, with clutter and clothes everywhere, the room clearly had some shortcomings. "I would describe the master bathroom as the armpit of our house," one owner says.

As the owners gradually discovered, looks can be deceiving. Though relatively spacious, their bathroom was poorly designed in terms of function, and over the years, that flaw led unavoidably to disorganization.

SITUATION

■ The bathroom offers more space than function. There's just one sink, and a rarely used soaking tub has become a black hole for clothes.

■ Existing closets fail to accommodate the owners' needs.

■ The room is too utilitarian.

SOLUTIONS

■ Gut the room. Remove the soaking tub and reconfigure the layout to gain space for an additional sink and a larger shower.

■ Expand storage options. Replace an overflowing closet with cabinets that offer easy access to belongings. Add a double vanity to gain more drawer and cabinet space.

■ Add style by painting the walls and introducing accessories. Warm up the room with rich wood-tone cabinetry.

ORDER RESTORED The standard-issue closet—a rod with a shelf above—didn't cut it in this house. The new system maximizes efficiency. In this section a rod is placed higher up to hold shirts, while a slide-out pants rack maximizes the space near the floor. Drawers are conveniently positioned for retrieving everyday items, such as socks. The inside of the door is outfitted with a mirror, a space-saving alternative to a freestanding floor-length model.

IN PROGRESS

BEFORE

DURING THE MAKEOVER Professional organizer Amy Rehkemper presents her remodeling and reorganization plan to the homeowners *above left, right*. **BEFORE THE MAKEOVER The large soaking tub** *above right* **had become a place to drop clothing.**

WORKING THE ROOM

A bigger bathroom may seem like everyone's dream, but professional organizer Amy Rehkemper isn't one to be swept away by square footage. "Having a big bathroom is just going to mean there's more stuff to put in it," she says. "It's not necessarily how big the room is, it's how you work the room."

And work the room she did. Her clutter-busting questions—"Do you use it?" "Do you love it?"—helped the owners realize that some serious work was ahead. A seldom-used soaking tub was first on the chopping block; it had to go. "It's deep and it's hard to get in and out of, so it makes a good clothes rack," one owner admits. Though they used the double closets, the owners didn't love them. The standard-issue rod with a shelf above didn't function for them, resulting in bathroom supplies and clothing that spilled all over. Similarly a single-sink vanity failed to serve their needs. The couple had to take turns grooming and had limited counter and cabinet space for their grooming gear.

Plastic storage containers and a hamper, brought in by the owners in a previous attempt to expand storage, had become obstacles to navigate around. "We need to get those items behind closed doors and in an organized fashion," Amy says.

POLISHED ACT Creative storage solutions for drawers are found in many places, including the kitchen-gadget aisle of most discount stores. This makeup organizer is actually a spice rack.

GREAT IMPOSTORS

Drawers can be a dumping ground for small things that culminate in a big mess. That's why professional organizer Amy Rehkemper is always on the lookout for smart storage solutions. "When you're getting containers and when you're going to outfit your own drawers, don't conform to what the package says you have to use," she says. "Always look for other ways to conquer a drawer." Consider her tricks and tips:

■ Use kitchen spice racks to organize fingernail polish, aspirin and tablets, and other items that come in small bottles or plastic containers. Spice racks can also be used inside medicine cabinets to elevate items. A metal spice rack may be stylish enough to be left out in the open as a corral for countertop clutter.

■ Recycle the trays from candy boxes; they come in a variety of shapes and sizes and are good for containing small items. Cup-style trays used for individual chocolates, for example, make nifty containers for earrings and cuff links.

■ Keep tweezers and other small metal objects from getting lost by sticking them on a magnet attached to the side of a drawer or a cabinet door.

STARTING OVER

Rather than put a bandage on their problem bath, the owners bought into Amy's plan for major surgery. The plan included replacing the stand-alone shower, soaking tub, single vanity, and closets with more functional pieces and reconfiguring the layout of the room. As the work progressed new opportunities emerged.

"It's hard to believe this whole thing started out of just reorganizing my sock drawer," one owner says. "One thing led to another, and the next thing you know, we've got this incredible bathroom space."

First came function: Adding a combination shower/tub opened up space for a double vanity, which provided much-needed counter space and cabinet storage. The ill-equipped closets gave way to a wall-spanning storage unit for jewelry, supplies, clothes, and more. Drawers that fully extend put all the contents in plain view. A pocket door slides into the wall to open up space for a storage cabinet in the entrance area.

EXTRA, EXTRA The corner where the shower used to be located is now open and stylish, with features not typically found in a utilitarian space. A built-in glass-fronted cabinet offers storage or display space, and the artwork in an ornate gilt frame is an elegant touch *above left*. The partial wall, trimmed with molding, creates a private area for the toilet without the claustrophobic feel of a water closet. Candles and a table lamp on the cabinet in the entrance area cast a warm glow on the room, perfect for a relaxing soak in the tub. **SPACE ECONOMY** This fashionable magazine rack *above right* makes the most of the limited space on the partial wall.

GRAND ENTRANCE A stylishly smart double vanity draws people into the bath and offers plenty of space for grooming. Before the makeover the first thing people saw upon entering was a lackluster single-sink vanity with a cluttered countertop. The mirror reflects more rich-looking cabinetry.

Second came looks: Rich wood cabinetry, new tile, and fresh paint lend an air of sophistication. Artwork and accessories take the room from utilitarian to homey.

And third came the lessons: To keep the bath looking ship-shape, Amy went deeper. In drawers she installed plastic storage bins that stack or slide across one another; these will keep different items from getting jumbled together. "Don't be afraid to combine categories [in one drawer], as long as there's a clear separation between the two," she says. Behind cabinet doors, she placed labeled bins and baskets to stow supplies and bathing essentials.

"I feel relaxed in here," one owner says of the tidy, spalike space. "It just feels good."

BEFORE THE MAKEOVER The closet shelves *above left* **were a cluttered mess of shampoo bottles, miscellaneous containers, and bathroom essentials. A single vanity** *above right* **meant the owners had to take turns grooming.**

BEHIND CLOSED DOORS Bathroom cabinetry that resembles fine furniture is a recent trend. With its rich wood tones and trimmed-out top, this built-in closet looks like a massive armoire. A mix of drawers, shelves, and rods for hanging clothes ensures a place for everything.

■□ **NAME THAT BASKET** Wicker baskets are a stylish way to contain items *above left*. Clear labels affixed to the
■■ edges of the shelves make identification easy, without being an eyesore. **SUPPLY CLOSET** Though the bath has a
spalike feel, reality sets in inside this cabinet with plastic bins that store cleaners and rags *above right*. The bin
designated for extra cleaning supplies makes it easy to remember where the stash is and to take a quick inventory.
Professional organizer Amy Rehkemper recommends storing the extra supplies with the in-use items (when possible) to
make it easy to determine what needs to be replenished.

INVEST WISELY

If you're investing in new cabinetry, put storage considerations at the
top of your list.

■ **Be flexible.** Adjustable shelves are a must. Choose storage options
that can keep pace with your needs.

■ **Size things up.** Drawers and shelves can be outfitted with many
extras; consider whether the investment is worth the cost and whether
the features will have long-term appeal. Paying for drawers that fully
extend, for example, is wasted money if your space is too narrow to
accommodate the full length of the drawer when it's pulled out. A
drawer with compartments for CDs could be rendered useless when
the next new technology comes along, and a drawer lined in velvet
might be an unnecessary splurge if your jewelry collection is minimal.

■ **Plan for the future.** It's a good idea to allow for a little extra
storage. (Think of how many times you've heard people say they wish
they had built their deck a bit larger, or they wish they had purchased
a house with a fourth bedroom.) Take a quick inventory to help you
plan ahead. If you have 10 towels, for example, choose a shelf that
will hold a stack of at least 20.

@ VISIT WWW.HGTV.COM/LABELS FOR EXCLUSIVE
LABELS YOU CAN PERSONALIZE.

VITAMINS

FACIAL MOISTURIZER

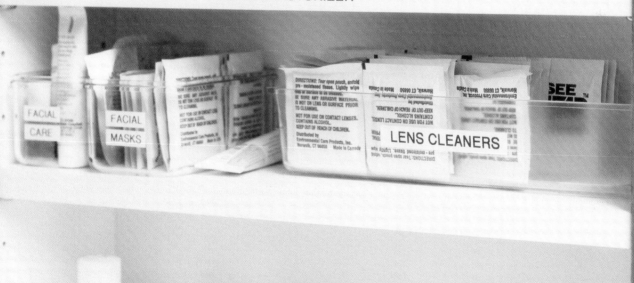

FACIAL CARE

FACIAL MASKS

LENS CLEANERS

 FLEX TO FIT Adjustable shelves make every inch count inside this cabinet, while labels and clear plastic bins make the contents easy to grab.

TWO SPACES ARE BETTER THAN ONE

PEOPLE OFTEN ASK ONE ROOM TO DO TOO MUCH—AND SOMETIMES CAREFUL PLANNING AND A SMART LAYOUT ALONE CANNOT MEET THE CHALLENGE. IN SUCH CASES IT PAYS TO UTILIZE TWO ROOMS FOR INCREASED FUNCTION.

At times almost every room in the home can feel like a multipurpose area; busy people squeeze many activities into their days—and into a single room. However, if you have the space available, calling two rooms into action can smooth the path to organizational success. Two rooms offer options, solutions, and flexibility that one room may not be able to match.

This section features two homes that each utilize dual rooms to maximize storage possibilities and increase functionality. The attic guest room and adjoining sitting room on page 166 offer guests a quiet place to relax during a visit; they also function as an everyday retreat for the homeowners. The crafts room and office on page 174 are filled with smart storage solutions to keep an avid stitcher and crafter organized. Together the two spaces allow her ample room to work; her husband finds space for his work and hobbies too.

TUCKED IN A bookcase maximizes the space under the eaves, corralling books near the entrance to the sitting room. A full-length mirror takes advantage of the partially propped-open door to offer guests a convenient spot to check their appearance. An iron and ironing board that formerly took up floor space are stowed on a rack on the other side of the door.

UNDER-THE-EAVES MAKEOVER

THIS ATTIC GUEST SUITE WAS PROOF THAT ITS OWNER HAD SHOPPED 'TIL SHE DROPPED. WITH BAGS EVERYWHERE, NO ROOM WAS LEFT FOR GUESTS. THANKS TO MAJOR SORTING AND SIMPLE STORAGE SOLUTIONS, THE SPACE IS NOW READY WHEN COMPANY CALLS—AND WHENEVER THE OWNER WANTS TO GET AWAY FROM IT ALL.

T he era of excess has caught up with many homes across the country. Almost everyone has at least one room that has too much of this, too much of that. Whenever this spendthrift returned home after a day of shopping, her path led straight to the attic guest suite. Shopping bags filled with clothes, gifts, and crafts buried the beds and floor and had turned the space into an unmentionable. "I was speechless," the husband recalls of a rare jaunt he made to the suite. The couple's children also avoided the area.

This wasn't a case of a shopping-crazed wife trying to hide things. "I was just putting it out of the way—just putting it up there until I could get organized with it," she says. That day had long passed, so professional organizer Crystal Sabalaske came to the rescue. "I don't want you to panic, because it's going to look worse in there before it gets better," she cautions. "Sometimes that happens with organizing. It's all part of the process."

BEFORE

SITUATION

- ◾ The two-room guest suite has turned into a dumping ground for one owner's purchases and crafts projects.

- ◾ The closet is disorganized, cramped, and difficult to navigate.

- ◾ Angled walls limit the types and placement of furnishings.

SOLUTIONS

- ◾ Toss unneeded items and organize what remains. Reclaim the space as a guest room and create a sitting room the owner can also enjoy.

- ◾ Improve the function and efficiency of the closet by using vertical storage space and removing one rod.

- ◾ Find creative solutions to maximize the awkward wall space.

ROOM AT THE INN Prior to this closet conversion, hangers virtually slapped the owner in the face when she opened the door. With the front rod removed, there's room to navigate and easily access the shelves on both ends of the closet; the cart that holds sweaters can be rolled out of the way. By pitching clothes she didn't wear and using vertical hanging space, such as tiered pants hangers, the owner found that the two remaining rods were adequate.

DUTIFUL DESK Filing cabinets topped with a countertop-style work surface create a thrifty desk *above left*. SWEET DREAMS Cleared of clutter, the yellow and blue bedding *above right* sends a cheery welcome to guests and to the owner when she makes the daily trek to the cedar closet. Fresh paint adds to the clean look, with the neutral color creating a spacious feel.

DIAGNOSE AND TAKE ACTION

Though the owner had already diagnosed herself as a shopaholic, Crystal added a new ailment: bag syndrome. "It's not medical terminology or anything," she says. "It's what I call my clients who have bags of stuff lying everywhere. The problem with bags and trying to organize stuff in bags is it's really difficult because you don't know what's in there."

What goes in must come out, in Crystal's view. "Before I start the organizing process, I take everything out of bags and take everything out of boxes," she says. "This is how it sometimes gets messier before it starts to look better."

Once everything was out in the open—even the jam-packed closet that housed the owner's clothes was emptied out—the sorting began. Crystal designated large plastic storage bins for sorting items into "keep," "donate," and "toss" categories. She also designated a "store elsewhere" pile for stray items. "We're not going to waste the time whenever we find something, running to that room to put it away, because that will cause us to lose focus," she says.

The pair also made quick work out of deciding what would stay and what would go. With so many items and so much clothing to sort through, a speedy approach was a necessity.

Though the owner says she's prepared to go cold turkey to kick her shopping habit, that extreme isn't the only answer. In fact Crystal has a better idea: "I actually give you permission to shop," she says. "You just need to get rid of some of your older items first to make room for the new items so that you don't end up with the shopping bag syndrome again. If you bring something new into the house, get rid of something that you don't wear anymore."

QUIET TIME The sitting area is a sea of tranquillity, with walls and fabrics in calming colors. A bed is purposefully placed out of view from the entrance so the room beckons people for reading and relaxing. The owner can also use the space to work on crafts projects.

A BROADER PURPOSE

To prevent the guest room from becoming dead space—something that's likely to happen if visitors aren't flocking in—Crystal broadened its function, making it into a retreat for the owner. The larger room remains the primary sleeping quarters for guests, and with the clutter removed it's fully guest-worthy. It's also an inviting place for the owner to plan her wardrobe and iron clothes. The adjoining room is now a sitting area where the owner can read, relax, or work on crafts projects.

Getting an under-the-eaves room to function well presents special challenges. Crystal solved them—and the storage issue—with ease. A bookshelf placed against an angled wall creates hidden storage space behind the shelf, bringing function to an area that was too low for any other purpose. Risers that cost less than $3 each elevate a bed in the sitting room, creating storage space underneath for the owner's crafts projects and not-yet-given gifts. An $11 rack mounts on the back of a door between the two rooms to hold an iron and ironing board, which previously hogged floor space.

Behind closed doors, the cedar closet is a tidy little sanctuary. After purging clothes she didn't wear and removing one of the three rods, the owner has room to move in the closet and can access shelves at each end. "I don't have to rummage through everything," she says. "Everything is in its place, and I love it."

HIDE-AND-SEEK Attics and other rooms with sloped walls are challenging to furnish—so challenging that the owner had simply hung a clothes rod where the angled ceiling started, doing her best to make use of the awkward space. Professional organizer Crystal Sabalaske made the most of the situation by butting a five-shelf unit up to the angled ceiling and using the gap created behind the shelf for storage of rarely needed items *top*. Baskets, plastic storage bins, and accessories placed on the shelves camouflage what's behind them. **BEFORE THE MAKEOVER** This attic suite was previously brimming with gifts yet to be given, clothing, and crafts projects *above left*. Gail O'Neill consults with the homeowners *above right* **before** professional organizer Crystal Sabalaske steps in to take over.

BEFORE

BEFORE

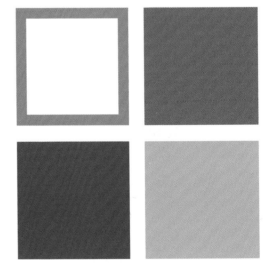

BEFORE THE MAKEOVER Clutter migrated from one portion of this attic suite to the other *top*. The cedar closet *above*—a wonderful bonus in any home—was so crammed with clothing that the owner had a difficult time navigating it and finding what she needed.

CLASSIFIED INFORMATION

In real estate the watchword is "location, location, location." In organizing it's "label, label, label." Taking a few extra minutes to identify the contents of boxes saves time later because you won't have to rummage through containers to find things. Consider these tips:

■ Invest in a label maker from an office supply store to make on-the-spot labels. Alternatively make your labels via a computer or use a black marker to handwrite them.

■ Test self-sticking labels to ensure they will adhere to the chosen storage container. Use clear mailing tape for extra durability and also to affix nonadhesive labels.

■ Check that the label can be easily read from a distance—say, when you're standing on the floor trying to figure out what's in a box on a high shelf. Choose heavy, bold fonts if generating the label from a computer. Use a thick black marker for handwritten labels.

■ For extra durability laminate nonstick labels. Laminated labels work especially well on storage containers that have slots the label can slide into. To attach labels to other types of containers, punch holes in the top corners of the label, thread the label with ribbon, and tie it to a handle or loop it through a woven basket to secure.

■ If you're labeling clear plastic containers that will be handled frequently, put the label inside the container, with the word(s) on the label facing outward. This will help the label last longer. Use clear mailing tape to affix the label to the container.

VISIT WWW.HGTV.COM/LABELS FOR EXCLUSIVE LABELS YOU CAN PERSONALIZE.

SHELVES ON LEFT (back to front)	SHELVES ON RIGHT (back to front)	BACK ROW (left to right)	FRONT ROW (left to right)	Sliding Drawers (top to bottom)
Top Shelf	**Top Shelf**			
Out of season shoes	Collectible dolls	Suits		
Handbags	Linens	Jackets (denim)	Scarves & belts	**1st Drawer**
Handbags		Vests	Pants	Cardigans
		Coats & raincoats	Skirts	
2nd Shelf	**2nd Shelf**	Long sleeve dresses	Blazers	**2nd Drawer**
In season shoes	Collectible dolls	Short sleeve shirts	Long sleeve blouses	Cardigans
Turtleneck sweaters	Travel bags	Sleeveless shirts	Fleece & flannels	
		Short sleeve dresses		**3rd Drawer**
				V-neck & crew neck sweaters
3rd Shelf	**3rd Shelf**	Sleeveless dresses		
Out of season shoes	Jena's memorabilia	Kid's clothing/Jena's dresses		
Jeans	Wedding dress	Halloween costumes		
Sweatshirts	Sewing machine	Furs		
	Wedding memories & accessories			
	Luggage/duffle bag			
Bottom Shelf (floor)	**Bottom Shelf (floor)**			
Out of season shoes	Jena & Phil's memorabilia			
Boots	Photos			
	Jena's memorabilia			
	Jean's memorabilia			

THIS WAY, PLEASE An inventory of the closet contents posted on the door takes labeling to the extreme—in a good way. "I want to make sure things are just as easy for you to put away as they are to retrieve," professional organizer Crystal Sabalaske says. The sign maps out specific shelves and rows in the closet that hold everything from raincoats and long-sleeve dresses to linens and collectible dolls.

Turtleneck Sweaters

SPINNING A YARN Fabric-lined baskets filled with yarn rest on shelves in the knitting area, taking advantage of vertical storage space. The adjustable shelves maximize storage capabilities. The countertop provides space for storing and using the knitting machine. Labeled drawers make it easy to find supplies and to return them to their designated areas.

general craft supplies

mailing supplies

buttons

buttons

CRAFTING A SOLUTION

ROOMS DESIGNED FOR CRAFTING PRESENT SPECIAL CHALLENGES. SCISSORS, GLUES, FABRICS, SEWING NOTIONS, AND MORE REQUIRE MULTIPLE KINDS OF STORAGE. THE OWNERS OF THESE ADJOINING ROOMS DIDN'T THINK THEY HAD SPACE TO HOLD IT ALL UNTIL PROFESSIONAL ORGANIZER DIANE ALBRIGHT INTRODUCED THEM TO SMART STRATEGIES FOR STREAMLINING AND SORTING.

Like many a hobbyist, this crafter had a home overflowing with stuff. Her obsession with all things fabric and yarn had spun out of control in the two rooms she used for her hobby, which was on the verge of becoming a burgeoning business. "I have to dig to find things, because I know I might have another piece of polka-dot fabric someplace, but who knows where?" she says.

Her husband was wary of entering the rooms where the sewing, knitting, and other handiwork was always in progress. "I'd love to be able to come down and use the computer, but at any given moment you can sit on a pin or a knitting needle," he says. "One never knows."

Though the couple envisioned a tidy space for the husband to use the computer or watch TV while the wife attended to her designs, professional organizer Diane Albright had different thoughts about calming the chaos. "You are trying to do too much in too small of a space," she says.

SITUATION

■ The crafter wastes valuable time clearing off work surfaces and looking for tools and materials for her projects.

■ The crafter has no system for keeping fabrics, yarns, sewing notions, patterns, and paperwork organized.

■ The clutter renders the television and computer virtually useless.

SOLUTIONS

■ Improve efficiency by designating areas for specific tasks, such as sewing, knitting, and cutting fabrics. Keep necessary tools and materials in their respective work areas.

■ Establish easy-to-maintain organizational systems. Inventory and categorize the fabrics, patterns, notions, and yarns and create a color-coded filing system for paperwork.

■ Create a separate office for the computer, television, and stereo equipment.

GIVE ROOMS A PURPOSE

Rather than attempt to create two dual-purpose spaces, Diane decided to assign each room a separate function. One room would be the production studio, while the other room would become an office that both owners could use.

The first order of business was to declutter and repurpose each space. The computer, television, and stereo equipment were dug out from the clutter and moved into the newly designated office. A cutting mat and other items were transferred from the office into the production studio. An old desk and chair were given to charity. With all the remaining items in their respective new homes, it was time to sort and categorize.

By their nature hobbies—be it sewing, collecting, or tinkering—can be tough to rein in. Diane's approach was to dive right into the mess, tackling one small area at a time and sorting items into four categories: put away, throw away, give away, and "another day"—the latter being a category Diane was hesitant to offer. "This is just for something you absolutely can't part with right now," she explains.

When the crafter seemed perplexed about two metal rings she came across, Diane offered advice: "If you can't tell in three seconds [what it is], you get rid of it." And when unfinished projects were discovered, Diane offered another maxim: Get rid of any unfinished projects that you haven't touched in the past six months.

ATTITUDE ADJUSTMENT New charcoal-color carpeting and the same bright yellow paint used in the crafts room update the office *above right*. The office contents were previously a jumbled mess in the crafts room *above left*. At $2,112 the desk and bookcase were a splurge. However, it was a sound investment that will help the creative owner organize the business side of her crafting and present a professional image to potential clients. The checked valance behind the desk conceals an air conditioner.

SPOOL TOOL A wall-mounted rack such as this is great for storing items that come on a spool, including thread, yarn, ribbon, string, and twine. Consider one for a crafts room, garage, or closet that's designated as a gift wrap station.

Serger Tools

Velcro Dots

BIAS
Tape Maker

IN THE CLEAR Stackable storage containers arranged on built-in shelves bring order to sewing notions, a collection of vintage buttons, and other small items. "These containers can be addictive," professional organizer Diane Albright says. The clear containers, which cost about $6 each, make it easy to identify the contents. When purchasing containers for small items, such as safety pins and buttons, check that the lids snap on tightly to prevent the contents from spilling.

SAY WHAT? CATCHPHRASES

Bring rhyme and reason to organizing with these mantras:

■ **When in doubt, throw it out.** If you're less than 100 percent sure that you'll use an item or that you need it— or if you don't even know what it is—get rid of it.

■ **Act like you're moving.** An impending move to a new house or apartment is always a great motivator for a decluttering mission. Set a fictional move date and use the time until then to get your belongings in order.

■ **Use it or lose it.** Whether it's a tie that hasn't been worn in a year or a pizza stone gathering dust in a kitchen cupboard, an unused item is only cluttering your home—and complicating your life every time you have to move it to find what you're after.

■ **Put apples with apples.** Grouping like items together makes it easy to remember where things are and encourages you to return items to their designated place. Assign every shelf, drawer, and cupboard a specific duty or specific contents. Think of it as giving a theme to each storage space.

EASY SOLUTIONS, LASTING RESULTS

The production studio wasn't able to accommodate piles of fabric for future projects, so those remained in the office. Diane brought order to the excess yardage, though, with a smart inventory system that makes quick work of finding a specific fabric. The fabric was sorted into categories by color, fabric type, and yardage and then placed in numbered baskets that were filed in order on the wall-mounted shelves. Swatches and key details of each fabric were then organized into plastic sleeves in a binder and assigned numbers that correspond to the baskets. After checking the binder, the crafter knows exactly where to find specific fabric.

Diane applied a similar approach to keep paperwork organized. To give the owners a visual cue and a strategy for organizing incoming papers, Diane designated yellow folders for reference materials and red folders for working files. "I wanted to keep it simple," she says of the two-color system.

STEP-BY-STEP

To make organizing less intimidating, take it in stages. Start by forming a mental picture of your overall home and assigning a purpose to each room. When you're ready to take action, concentrate on one room. Remove items that distract from the primary purpose of the room, such as coats draped over kitchen chairs or a briefcase next to a bed. Gradually the clutter will be cleared and it won't seem so daunting to get the rest of the room in order. Leave the items in a temporary holding spot until you finish the room. Then put the items away in their proper spots.

TAKE INVENTORY Though some of the owner's sewing items spilled over into the office, professional organizer Diane Albright brought logic to it. This wall of shelves stores fabrics in baskets that are numbered and shelved numerically. Fabric swatches are stored in binder sleeves, accompanied by the number of the basket that holds each larger fabric piece. Sleeves designed to hold computer disks work well for fabric swatches, paint chips, and other small, flat items.

ESTABLISH A CREATIVE ENVIRONMENT

To keep the crafter's creative juices flowing and to visually connect the two rooms, Diane chose a bold yellow paint for the walls. The yellow is an equally invigorating alternative to the bright pink that was in one of the rooms and has the advantage of being gender-neutral. Black accents anchor the scheme. The storage containers, including black magazine holders and black and white toile boxes, were chosen to complement the decor.

Carefree creative types and organized spaces rarely go hand in hand, yet Diane believes the two can mesh. "We take the person's style and his or her needs and work with that," she says. "It can be done."

The crafter agrees that the rooms look, feel, and function better without compromising her love of color or stifling her creativity. "Everything is where I need it," she says. "I don't have to dig."

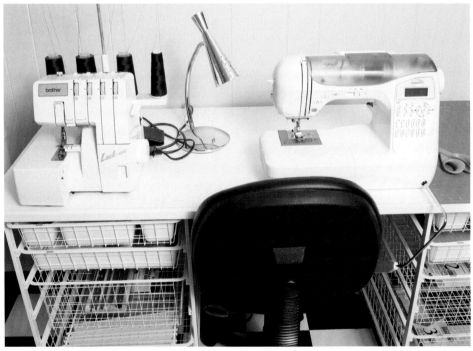

SEWN UP The tidy sewing station *above* features wire drawers, some outfitted with storage containers, that keep scissors and other necessities within reach. Hanging folders keep sewing-related guides accessible. **BEFORE THE MAKEOVER** The crafts room *above left* and the adjoining room, which is now the newly designated office *below left*, were overflowing with fabric, unfinished crafts projects, and patterns.

COLOR CONNECTIONS Playing off the checked floor, black accents "pop" against the yellow walls. The storage containers and magazine holders blend into the black shelf. A wall-mounted cabinet keeps the ironing board safe from clutter pileup. If you can't sacrifice wall space, consider an over-the-door ironing board rack.

IN THE BAG If you've got it, flaunt it. Handcrafted bags that were formerly scattered about the crafts room and over the television become wall art in the office. Even if you don't have to impress clients with your handiwork, a collection of vintage purses, hats, or children's clothing makes an intriguing display when suspended from inexpensive metal hooks.

STORAGE SMARTS

When you vow to store items out of sight or tidy things up, resist the urge to quickly dump them into a box. Proper storage is key to the longevity of nearly any item.

■ Avoid hanging clothing in plastic bags, such as those from the dry cleaner. These bags don't let the garments breathe and can cause mildew to form, especially during the summer months. Invest in fabric garment bags instead.

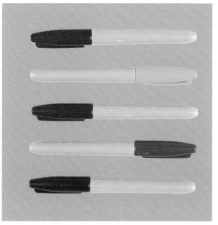

■ The bathroom seems like a logical place to store medicines. However, capsules and tablets are actually better stored in a moisture-free environment. Remove the cotton plug after opening the container; if it's left in, moisture can form inside the bottle. Keep medicines in their original containers; save the cute pillboxes and other containers for travel purposes only, and use them only if you're unable to bring the original container.

■ To prevent shoes made of fabric or another pliable material from losing their shape, lightly stuff them with tissue paper or newspaper.

■ Keep unused blankets from gathering dust by storing them in a king-size pillowcase or a zippered bag from a bedspread. Similarly use a pillowcase to store folded-up sheet sets. When it's time to change the bedding, everything you need is in the pillowcase, so you won't have to rummage through the shelves.

RESOURCES

PAGES 70-79

Episode: 410

Designer: Mela Catanzaro, Mela Catanzaro Interiors, mela@mcatinteriors.com, www.mcatinteriors.com.

Resources: *Paint:* Frostwork SW0059, Hubbard Squash SW0044, Downing Straw SW2813, Extra White SW7006, Dover White SW6385, Sherwin-Williams, 800-331-7979, www.sherwin-williams.com. *Scooter office lamp, bulletin board, Sonoma hutch, monitor stand, mesh desk chair, two-drawer mesh file cart, CD case steel:* Stacks and Stacks Housewares, 800-761-5222, www.stacksandstacks.com. *Wall/desk light, three nesting tables, revolving bookcase, storage cube:* Brookstone, 800-846-3000, www.brookstone.com. *Pandan storage stool, pushpins, storage chest, chest dividers, five case totes, stacking drawers, CD organizer, hanging file folders, file folders, bookends, magazine file, Jute canvas boxes, tray table, Makati oval wastebasket, Makati CD basket, seamless tins, desk leg, Zen notice board, mesh magazine file, shantung photo box, stapler, desk pad, pencil cupholder, drawer organizer, letter tray:* The Container Store, 888-CONTAIN (266-8246), www.containerstore.com. *Table:* Hydra Designs, Inc., 201-583-0800, www.hydradesigns.com.

PAGES 80-87

Episode: 301

Designer: Vicki Norris, Restoring Order, 888-625-5774 (Organizational Services), 877-625-5774 (Product Ordering), Info@RestoringOrder.com, www.RestoringOrder.com.

Resources: *Garage unit:* GarageTek, 866-664-2724, www.garagetek.com. *Flooring:* Racedeck, 800-457-0174, www.racedeck.com.

PAGES 88-95

Episode: 308

Designer: Crystal Sabalaske, cluttershrink, crystal@cluttershrink.com, www.cluttershrink.com.

Resources: *Storage cube, Space Bags, Portofino letterboxes, one navy and one cappuccino, cotton 20-Pocket overdoor shoe bag, square Pandan wastebasket, eight-drawer storage chest, short small Akro bin, long small blue Akro bin, wide white medium Akro bin, Truberry Calypso Toy Trolly, red Shantung photo box, blue Shantung photo box, five-drawer storage chest, clear Busy Box, medium tote, Gameboard Box, mesh cubes, EVA storage stool, stacking storage box and lid, stacking storage casters, red and blue half stowaway boxes, platinum Elfa desk legs, beech Elfa veneer desktop:* The Container Store, 888-CONTAIN (266-8246), www.containerstore.com. *Four-panel fabric floor screen, Medusa floor light, iris Medusa table light, 74-quart storage box, cherry magazine rack:* Stacks and Stacks Housewares, 800-761-5222, www.stacksandstacks.com. *Natural Cherry Connect the Dots Tables:* Levenger Company, 800-667-8034, www.levenger.com. *Handwoven fern trunks, canisters, scoops, fabric-lined baskets:* Lillian Vernon, 800-545-5426, www.lillianvernon.com. *Four-drawer tower with casters, three-drawer mini chests, 18-gallon containers, DVD/VHS organizers, 16-gallon tub with handles, slim single drawers, 3-gallon containers,*

1.5-gallon containers, 16.5-gallon container: Rubbermaid Home Products, 888-895-2110, www.rubbermaid.com. *Saddle Simply Suede sofa and love seat covers, Indigo Denim sofa cover, 23" red cotton Duck Floor pillow, 4'10"x7'10" Inca rug, 17" mocha Knife Edge Visions pillow, Simply Suede 17" box pillow:* Sure Fit Inc., 888-754-7166, www.surefit.net. *Maple bookshelf:* Smart Furniture, 888-467-6278, www.smartfurniture.com. *Table Bed:* Inova LLC, 866-528-2804, www.inovallc.com.

PAGES 96–105

Episode: 412

Designer: Vicki Norris, Restoring Order, 888-625-5774 (Organizational Services), 877-625-5774 (Product Ordering), Info@RestoringOrder.com, www.RestoringOrder.com.

Resources: *Desk:* Top Shelf Closet Company, Inc., 610-469-6689, www.topshelfclosets.com. *Paint:* Cajun Red SW0008, Empire Gold SW0012, and Sheraton Sage SW0014, Sherwin Williams, www.sherwin-williams.com. *Action Centers (five-tray paper sorter), Project Centers (bleachered file stand), Essentials Centers (four-drawer supply organizer), Drawer Dividers (drawer organizers), Rubbish Bins (garbage can), Journal Cases (magazine holders):* Restoring Order, 888-625-5774, www.RestoringOrder.com.

PAGES 108–117

Episode: 408

Designer: Genevieve Snyder, Genevieve Fine Art & Consulting, Genevieve.snyder@verizon.net

Resources: *Clean Park car mats:* Stacks and Stacks Housewares, 800-761-5222, www.stacksandstacks.com. *Ceiling storage shelves:* Garage Outfitters, 512-261-3865, www.garage-outfitters.com. *FreedomRail garage system and activity baskets:* Schulte Corp., 800-669-3225, www.schultestorage.com.

PAGES 118–125

Episode: 406

Designer: Sean Johnson, Organized Bliss™, sean@organizedbliss.org, www.organizedbliss.org.

Resources: *Country bench:* Improvements, 800-642-2112, www.improvementscatalog.com. *Maize storage trunks, picket-fence bookcase, willow baskets with red liners, rolling double hamper, monogrammed denim bean bag chairs, set of three lined baskets:* Lillian Vernon, 800-545-5426, www.lillianvernon.com. *Art supply cart:* Bellacor, 877-723-5522, www.bellacor.com. *Storage boxes:* Rubbermaid Home Products, 888-895-2110, www.rubbermaid.com. *Porcelain Beige Tuscan Valley Tiles, 6x6:* Mannington Mills, Inc., 856-935-3000, www.mannington.com. *Closet installation:* Top Shelf Closet Company, Inc., 610-469-6689, www.topshelfclosets.com. *Bookends, interlocking drawer organizers, flip boxes, jumbo clear box, clear sweater box, Makati basket, blue portfolio, jute box:* The Container Store, 888-CONTAIN (266-8246), www.containerstore.com.

PAGES 126–133

Episode: 211

Designer: Janet Taylor, Professional Organizer, Totally Organized, LLC, 215-229-7232, jtaylor@totallyorganized.biz, www.totallyorganized.biz. Deana O. Murphy, ASID Allied, Interior Designer, LivingDesigns Associates, LLC, 570-894-1166 dmurphy@livingdesignsassociates.com, www.livingdesignsassociates.com.

Resources: *Computer station, armoire, white dresser, wood rancher's lamp, white double-door desk, chest, primary bookcase, transportation clock, sport throw pillows, basketball rug:* Lillian Vernon, 800-545-5426, www.lillianvernon.com. *Shelf cabinet, drawer cabinet, cube cabinet, drawer cube, rolling pant trolley, tie hanger, hangers:* Stacks and Stacks Housewares, 800-761-5222, www.stacksandstacks.com. *Folding two-step stool, clear box:* Rubbermaid Home Products, 888-895-

2110, www.rubbermaid.com. *Paint:* Blazing Orange 2011-20, Patriot Blue 2064-20, Champagne Kisses 1240, Cinnamon 2174-20: Benjamin Moore, 800-672-4686, www.benjaminmoore.com. *Cottage kitchen pine chairs, ivory twin flat sateen sheet, ivory pillowcases:* L.L. Bean Inc., 800-441-5713, www.llbean.com. *Painting services:* Jenna DeFalco, Inspired Design LLC, idesign03@comcast.net.

PAGES 136–145

Episode: 401

Designer: Betty Kim, Betty's Room, LLC, betty@bettysroom.com, www.bettysroom.com.

Resources: *Paintable ceramic rectangle wall light:* Bellacor, 877-723-5522, www.bellacor.com. *Trash can, magazine holders, drawer dividers, clear box (mini), storage boxes, tray divider, underbed storage, display boxes, desk, shelving, chair, wire turtles, bulletin board, storage stool, paper sorter:* The Container Store, 888-CONTAIN (266-8246), www.containerstore.com. *Happy Eyes floor lamp, flex neck halogen table lamp:* Brookstone, 800-846-3000, www.brookstone.com. *Filing folders:* Pendaflex, www.pendaflex.com. *White cordless blinds cellular 54"x31":* Levolor Blinds, 770-460-0593. *Sage cotton craft duvet and sham, sage and blue faux suede pillows:* Textile Shop, 877-839-7467, www.textileshop.com. *Paint:* Sha Green, Tempistar, Analytical Green, White: Sherwin-Williams, 800-331-7979, www.sherwin-williams.com. *Solid Ground carpet squares, Citron, Mist, Chalk:* InterfaceFLOR, 866-281-3567, www.interfaceflor.com. *Clothes hangers:* Hangers.com, 800-400-6680, www.hangers.com. *Closet system installation:* Top Shelf Closet Company, Inc., 610-469-6689, www.topshelfclosets.com.

PAGES 146–153

Episode: 110

Designer: Maxwell Gillingham-Ryan, Apartment Therapy, info@apartmenttherapy.com, www.apartmenttherapy.com.

Resources: *Paint:* Rumba Orange Tinted, China White, White Dove, Benjamin Moore, 800-672-4686, www.benjaminmoore.com. *Natural Pandan storage stool 14¼"x17½", Orange Calypso rectangular boxes, medium gray storage box 11"x15"x6½", natural Pandan square nested boxes, natural XL magazine file 6"x10"x12½", natural hanging file box, Elfa platinum easy hang-top tracks, five-package wall anchors for ½" or ⅝" drywall, Elfa platinum hang standards, Elfa platinum shelves, ten-package Elfa shelf pins, six-pack Elfa galvanized shelf joiners, Beech veneer shelves:* The Container Store, 888-CONTAIN (266-8246), www.containerstore.com. *36-inch round table with adjustable height:* Hydra Designs, Inc., 201-583-0800, www.hydradesigns.com.

PAGES 154–163

Episode: 212

Designer: Amy Rehkemper, Simplify Organizing, LLC, 410-661-6248, amy@simplifyorganizing.com, www.simplifyorganizing.com.

Resources: *Paint:* Muresco Ceiling White, Fresh Start 100 percent acrylic primer, Providence Olive HC-98 flat, #1520, Benjamin Moore, 800-672-4686, www.benjaminmoore.com. *Shoe drawer, shoe bin, wire pull-out recycling basket, trays, necklace organizer, drawer organizers, clear boxes, folding skirt hanger, mesh bins, sweater boxes, shower caddy, easy liners, mesh laundry bag, EVA storage stool, tie and belt rack:* The Container Store, 888-CONTAIN (266-8246), www.containerstore.com. *Tub and plumbing fixtures:* Kohler Company, 800-456-4537, www.kohlerco.com. *Ceramic floor tiles:* Conestoga Tile, 717-564-6860, www.conestogatile.com. *Vanity tops:* DuPont Corian, 800-426-7426, www.corian.com. *Cabinetry:* Wood-Mode Fine Custom Cabinetry, 570-374-2711, www.wood-mode.com.

PAGES 166–173

Episode: 304

Designer: Crystal Sabalaske, cluttershrink, crystal@cluttershrink.com, www.cluttershrink.com.

Resources: *Legal storage boxes, photo storage boxes, Elfa casters, runner frame, runner drawers, drawer liners, drawer in/out stops:* The Container Store, 888-CONTAIN (266-8246), www.containerstore.com. *Maple-finish book shelf:* Smart Furniture, 888-467-6278, www.smartfurniture.com. *Cape Charles armchair, Cape Charles ottoman, Miranda nightstand, Medici adjustable desk lamp, velvet beaded pillows in sage and gold:* Pier 1 Imports, 800-245-4595, www.pier1.com. *Deluxe five-tier skirt open-end slack clothes hanger, Slimline hanger sets for women's clothing, Space Bag clothing bags, notched clothes hangers, ironing organizer, snap cases, swing-arm floor light, riser-bed elevators, straw totes, drawer chest, armoire wardrobe:* Stacks and Stacks Housewares, 800-761-5222, www.stacksandstacks.com. *Clear boxes with lids:* Rubbermaid Home Products, 888-895-2110, www.rubbermaid.com.

PAGES 174–185

Episode: 409

Designer: Diane Albright, organize@AllBrightIdeas.com, www.AllBrightIdeas.com.

Resources: *Two-tier junk drawer organizer, desk organizers, clear cube of drawers, chrome basket with handles, chrome basket without handles, Colonial candle:* All Bright Ideas, 866-632-8911, www.AllBrightIdeas.com. *Desk lamp:* Bellacor, 877-723-5522, www.bellacor.com. *Small, medium, and large clear containers:* Click Clack Limited, 800-884-4543, www.clickclack.com. *Desk with bookcase:* Lizell, 800-718-8882, www.lizell.com. *Hanging file folders, box-bottom hanging folders, interior manila file folders:* Pendaflex, www.pendaflex.com. *Binders, Office in the Round (carousel with office supplies), white square nesting boxes, desktop file, drawing box/accessory collection, circular nesting boxes, Classic Square Box, Classic Letterbox, Let's Get Started Set:* Russell and Hazell, 888-254-5837, www.russellandhazel.com. *Knitting-area workstation, desktop with basket for sewing equipment, shelving for patterns, shelving for fabric:* Schulte Corp., 800-669-3225, www.schultestorage.com. *Fold-away ironing board, hooks:* Stacks and Stacks Housewares, 800-761-5222, www.stacksandstacks.com. *Set of three baskets, set of five fabric boxes:* Storage Decor, 877-332-6726, www.storagedecor.com.

INDEX

to some, inspiration comes naturally.
for the rest of us, may we suggest a good book?

Make that three good books. In all three, including the popular *Before & After Decorating* and *Design on a Dime,* you'll find simple and affordable design ideas, not to mention plenty of inspiration from HGTV's expert designers. The newest addition, *Sensible Chic,* uses side-by-side comparisons to show how you can imitate a high-end room on a bargain budget.

YOU SHOULD SEE WHAT'S ON HGTV

HGTV.com